A CHILD
OF THE GHETTO

BENJAMIN GARBER, MD

ISBN: 978-0-578-85415-1

Cover Illustration: Timothy Foss
Cover Design & Book Layout: Summer R. Morris, Sumo Design Studio
Author Photo: Wylie Garber
Editor: Cynthia Zigmund
Editorial Services: Second City Publishing, LLC

Printed in the United States of America.

DEDICATION

*To my wife and children, who knew and
understood what I've been through.*

CONTENTS

INTRODUCTION

In the spring of 2020, my three daughters approached me and said just how much they enjoyed hearing me speak at psychiatric meetings and conferences. They also enjoyed hearing about my writing and watching me present scientific papers at psychiatric meetings. Even though they could not always understand what I was talking about they could tell that attendees paid attention to me and found what I had to say useful.

Because I am a Holocaust survivor, my daughters felt that I should include my Holocaust experiences in an autobiography. They knew that I appeared in a video for Steven Spielberg in 1997, but they felt that writing about my experiences would be more a personal, detailed, and meaningful record. When I asked just who I would write this for, they responded that it would be for me, for them, and perhaps a wider audience. They emphasized that any literature related to the Holocaust should be treasured and preserved for future generations.

I agree. This is my story.

A CHILD

OF THE

GHETTO

MY STORY

PART ONE

1

ORIGINS

(1936-1939)

WHEN AUTHORS APPROACH THE TOPIC of origins, they
invariably begin with their mother. My mother was considered a "bat
Ichida," which means an only daughter—more literal current translation
would be "a Jewish princess." My mother's Jewish name was Leah; she had
it changed to Lisa. She had a great love and a high regard for Poland and
the Polish people, an infatuation I do not share with her. It was always a
mystery how it was that my mother considered herself a part of the upper
stratum of Jewish society of Wilno, at least socially. The city of Wilno
had a large Jewish population (60,000 out of 200,000 citizens) so it was
difficult to determine where one belonged in the social order.[1] There may
have been several strands that came together to help her form such an all-

---

1   Vilnius is the current name of the city of Wilno. It is the capital of Lithuania and has a
population of 560,000 people. I chose to use the name Wilno because that was the Polish and the
Jewish name for the city. Vilnius is the Lithuanian name while Wilna was the German name. The
current population is primarily Lithuanian with some Poles and Russians.

pervasive impression. First, it was the city itself. Wilno was considered the seat of Jewish culture, religious fervor, and Jewish literature and creativity in Eastern Europe. Wilno was labeled "Yerushalayim de Lite" meaning Jerusalem of Lithuania. My mother took pride in that as she was born, raised, and educated in Wilno. Secondly, she completed Gymnasium, the equivalent of a college education. Although she was not a scholar, she took pride in having completed a higher-level education. She also studied the piano and was quite proficient. Her favorite composers were Chopin and Paderewski, both Polish. In later years, piano was an important aspect of who she was. Finally, her parents and my father's parents were wealthy Jewish merchants—her parents in meats and sausage, and my father's parents in lumber. She invariably let people know her origins and automatically assumed that anyone from the Wilno area must have heard of "Glasser of Sausage." Glasser, the Yiddish name for glassmaker, was my mother's maiden name.

My mother had two brothers, one older and one younger. Her older brother, Heshke, was the family star as he was a brilliant law student. He was also a highly regarded athlete. Because he was my grandmother's favorite, he and my mother were very competitive. Her younger brother, Elke, worked in my grandparents' sausage factory and was considered a hell-raiser. There were constant issues surrounding his partying and womanizing. He was not an intellectual giant.

I have seen pictures of my grandfather in which he appears as a hard and stern patriarch. My mother adored him, and he reciprocated the feeling. The boys attempted to rebel against him, without much success. My only connection to him is a family myth related to his smoking. He was a heavy cigarette smoker and when I was born in 1936, he swore at my birth that he would never smoke again. However, the vow was too late and he died from lung cancer before the beginning of World War II. I do not remember him. So, the two most important men in my early life, my father (who disappeared when I was two and a half years old) and my grandfather, are a total blank. Except for a few photographs, they have never existed in my consciousness.

From my perspective the key star in the family constellation was my grandmother, my mother's mother, whom I loved and adored. In the early years of my life my grandmother raised me. It seemed like my mother was never around, but my grandmother was always there. My mother would not disagree with that assessment.

My grandmother was depressed from the beginning of the war, the result of her sons having been snatched away by the police within a brief time span. Consequently, she devoted all her energy into caring for and raising me. She was a short, attractive, somewhat stocky woman who always had a fixed sad expression on her face. She was quiet and self-contained and even when participating in ongoing battles with my mother she never raised her voice. I am convinced that whatever stability I achieved in the early years of my development was due to my grandmother's attention and had little to do with my mother's presence. My grandmother's name was Riva; my oldest daughter is named after her.

When the war started and my father left with the Polish army, my mother and I stayed at my grandmother's house, which became a part of the Wilno Ghetto.[2] I do not remember much of that house except for a

---

2   The city of Wilno became a part of Poland in 1922 and, as stated in footnote one, is now known as Vilnius. It had a population of 220,000 people, mostly Poles, Jews, and Lithuanians. Wilno had a Jewish population of 70,000 people before the Holocaust—1,300 survived by hiding in buildings and the surrounding forests. The Ghetto existed from 1941-1943.

huge grandfather clock in the dining room that always chimed. As she was part of a work party that left the Ghetto in the morning and came home in the evening, my mother was gone all the time. She was conscripted for the work party; this was not by choice. She was making heavy boots for German soldiers who were freezing in the Russian Steppes. Even when my mother was around, she was always up to something. What that mysterious something was I did not figure out until years later. I did realize that my grandmother did not approve of my mother's activities, but the specifics escaped me. There were frequent battles between the two after which my mother would stomp out in a huff. Where she disappeared to, we never knew; upon returning, she stayed silent.

Although I was able to construct a viable picture of my mother's history and background, I did not experience such luxury when it came to my father. When the subject was my father there emerged a shadow or perhaps a hole, which I spent most of my life trying to fill, but never quite succeeded. What I learned about him emerged in my later years but even that was vague and sketchy. To compound the loss, my mother wrapped him in a shroud of silence so at times I doubted if such a person ever existed. I do not remember anything about him, and I have no memories to attach to the person. I have seen pictures but that is the extent of our connection. His parents were wealthy and successful lumber merchants in Wilno—the connection of both families was a highly desirable match. I imagine that the matchmaker collected a handsome fee for her efforts. What I know about my father's parents is nonexistent as I am unable to recall what they looked like or when they were killed.

While the coming together of both families seemed successful, I doubt that my parents had a happy marriage. The union sounded highly tempestuous—both individuals were strong-willed and assertive. My grandmother alluded to these negative qualities of both of my parents during her battles with my mother. My mother was tough and aggressive; my father had a temper. My hunch is that my father wanted children, while my mother had no interest in such a project. My mother did not want to be a mother. She demonstrated this by her words and actions. My father's name was Jonah Markman, the oldest of four (a sister and two brothers). What is so interesting about his siblings is that all three survived the Holocaust and eventually all three lived in Israel. I am assuming that the survival instincts of the Markman family were quite strong. As a result, I have a number of cousins and second cousins in Israel with whom I have maintained contact, albeit sporadic.

My mother always told me how smart my father was. He was a very successful lawyer in Poland, which was an almost impossible achievement for a Jew. He was an excellent student and extremely ambitious, but that is the extent of my knowledge regarding his character and abilities. I wish that I knew more about his personality.

Even the particulars of his death was an open question as one source told me that he was killed by the German troops that swept through Poland during the first two weeks of September 1939. However, one of my uncles recalled hearing that he was killed by the Russians at the Katyn Forest Massacre in Belarus in 1941.[3] Since he was an officer in the Polish Army I did a search at the Polish Museum in Chicago on Katyn Forest

---

3   In 1940, Stalin ordered the execution of 22,000 Polish officers and intellectuals in the Katyn Forest near the city of Smolensk in Belarus. This was done after Russia and Germany had divided Poland. At first the Russians blamed the massacre on the Nazis. However, with the acceptance of Glasnost they admitted responsibility.

victims and survivors. Checking out the Polish museum was a worthwhile undertaking since Chicago has a huge Polish population. However, I did not find his name of the list of Katyn victims, which has remained incomplete. There has been a palpable lack of cooperation on this issue among Poland, Russia, and the Polish community in Chicago. They seem to be fighting World War II all over again. Having read about it and studied it in some detail I doubt that the Katyn issue will ever be resolved.

Katyn is historically notorious since the Russians murdered 22,000 Polish officers and intellectuals when they split Poland with the Germans. Even though the Russians and the Poles have attempted to reconcile about what happened at Katyn and the Russians reluctantly admitted their guilt after blaming it on the Germans, it remains unresolved. To this day the issue of what happened, why it happened, and who is to blame has not been settled. Attempts at reconciliation have failed. Several years ago, a group of Polish dignitaries was on the way to Russia to sign a settlement between the countries, but the plane crashed in Belarus and there were no survivors. Katyn has been labeled as an unresolved sore from the history of World War II. My point in all this is that I will never know where and when my father died.

One of my uncles on my father's side, Ben Zion, was also in the Wilno Ghetto; he escaped, but because he and my mother did not get along, I am not sure how. Before the war he studied electrical engineering in France and later had a successful electrical engineering business in Israel with my other uncle, Joseph. Initially, Ben Zion was an electrical engineer at the Rutenberg Electrical Power Station on the Jordan River in Israel. He was captured by the Jordanians early during the 1948 War of Liberation and later released in a prisoner exchange. When I was in the Displaced Persons Camp in Germany from 1947-1949, he and I corresponded. He sent me Hebrew books, which I devoured. Most of the books were about the Irgun and the Stern Group, right wing extremists whose mission was to overthrow the British Government. I sympathized with those views and so I nurtured fantasies of going to Israel to help fight the British occupiers.

Ben Zion's daughter Daphna and I became close and we have gotten together when she visits the United States with her husband to attend conferences related to her work. She is in the same line of work as I—she is an art therapist. Daphna is bright and we have had some interesting conversations about self-psychology. Over the years she and I have exchanged psychiatric papers that we have written.

I finally got my wish to visit Israel as an adult. I spent time with my Uncle Joseph when I was in Israel for the first time. My wish to go there was nurtured by my all-consuming desire to experience the country and to reconnect with my father's family. I thought that Joseph would have the most information since he seemed the most knowledgeable about my father's history. I had many questions about my father's personality and his whereabouts, but Joseph was unable to answer most of them. Nevertheless, meeting him in Israel for the first and only time during that trip in the spring of 1971 was one of the most significant encounters of my life. I did not tell him that I was coming. I showed up with my wife, two children at the time, and David Garber, my stepfather's nephew. We waited for him at the office of his electrical company. He kept looking at me quizzically and asked if he was supposed to know me? I told him, "I am Benjamin from the United States." He was startled and we fell into each other's arms. He remembered my nickname, Momka, and realized the connection and that he had not seen me in thirty years. While our meeting was momentous, I also got to know his second wife, Hannah (Joseph was divorced from his first wife), who visited us many years after his death. I regretted not introducing myself as Benjamin, Jonah's son; looking back it felt disloyal to my father's memory. We also got to know his and Hannah's two children, David and Pnina, my cousins, with whom I have maintained sporadic contact. We traveled all over the Galilee, getting to know each other somewhat. Uncle Joseph told me that some of my facial expressions (including how I pursed my lips) and my long legs were similar to my father. Two years later when I went back to Israel, Joseph was dead and my questions remained unanswered. I was not aware that he had a history of chronic heart disease. He was the only one who was sure that my father was murdered at Katyn, but how he knew that was not clear.

The reason that this encounter was so significant was that I finally had living proof that I had a father and that he wasn't some ghost that I invented in my loneliness. Here was proof that there was this person to whom I was intimately connected even though I did not know him. Here was this person that I resembled. My oldest daughter honored my father and me by naming her first-born Jonah. For this and many other reasons, I adore my grandson Jonah.

I know the least about my Aunt Rivka, who escaped to Israel sometime after the beginning of World War II. She married and had two boys. I only knew this because of pictures that my mother received from her when we were in in the Displaced Persons camp in Germany. She died from uterine cancer at a very young age. My Uncle Joseph became the guardian of her boys and raised them. I met them during that first visit to Israel. The older one, Moshe, developed brain cancer and died at a young age.

The reason that I went into some detail about my father's siblings was an indirect attempt to learn more about him since I knew so little. All these efforts, while seemingly meaningful, did not fill the empty space that was my father.

There were many things that I would have asked my father: his relationship with my mother, what his parents were like, did he like being a lawyer, what he thought about Poland and its people since I had such mixed feelings about the country and its inhabitants.

2

BEGINNINGS

(1939-1941)

FROM MY TRAINING IN PSYCHIATRY, especially psychoanalysis, I learned that a person's earliest memories are often significant indicators of their earliest conflicts and anxieties. The accuracy of the remembered material is not that significant—it is the internal consistency and how these incidents fit with the rest of the narrative that ultimately determines its meaning. The responses and attitudes of early caretakers that permeate these early memories may be equally revealing in understanding a person's character formation. While these memories may be useful in and of themselves, they may be equally significant in that they piggyback with memories later in life. They may become significant markers that set the tone for future developmental issues. For example, it may be significant that my parents were never a part of my earliest memories. After all, my father was gone from my life when I was just two and a half years old, and my mother was never around. Therefore, it is not surprising that my

11

earliest memories focused on substitute caretakers. All that I have from my father are a few generalized facts and a couple of grainy photographs.

One of my earliest memories is from age two and a half or three. I was in the kitchen of our house with my nanny. She was a large Polish woman who was in her late forties or fifties. She was wearing a light blue flowered dress and a white apron. She was trying to get me to eat oatmeal, which I was resisting. She got me to do it by telling me that at the bottom of the bowl there was a picture of a big, beautiful stork and that if I finished my food, I would get to see it. It must have worked because I did see the stork, yet instead of being pleased, I was disappointed. I wonder if the image of the stork had something to do with my concern about having a sibling. Ever since then I have had a visceral dislike for oatmeal.

One of the hallmarks of my personality has been an automatic negative response to a demand coupled with an ever-present wish to please, which usually has mixed results. These polarities have always been at odds with one another. At times they have been useful qualities because it makes me seem compliant but just as often, they have gotten me into difficult situations.

As I go back into history to tell my story, especially when recalling traumatic incidents, I cannot help but wonder how many of these events in conjunction with other aspects of my personality have contributed to a chronic mild state of ever-present anxiety.

My mother had a special talent for saying things and making comments in an attempt to make me feel guilty. To provoke guilt was an ever-present attempt to control me when the usual methods were not successful. I must admit that she was competent at doing this, often in response to my misbehavior, whether real or imagined. These comments were painful, and I usually tolerated them in silence. It was not until years later—after psychoanalysis four days a week for four and a half years—that I developed useful emotional tools to defend myself.

My mother never failed to remind me that I was a sickly child while growing up; she was constantly taking me to doctors. I had a chronic stomach problem with frequent episodes of diarrhea, which she tried to minimize with a restricted diet. While my mother complained about my being sick all the time she would also brag about my compliance with dietary restrictions. The stomach issues may have been a significant problem early in my childhood; however, it has never been a problem since. The purpose of such recurrent reminders was to impress upon others (and me) what a devoted mother she was and what a burden I was. I must have been three or four at the time. I remember that, when we were leaving the doctor's office during this time, German airplanes appeared suddenly and it began to rain bombs. All I remember was running down the street with my mother and nanny and the surrounding sounds of explosions. It was a beautiful summer day, which suddenly turned gray and foreboding.

My next memory is from age four. This memory is extremely detailed and vivid. It has also been recurrent and so it has special meaning in the narrative of my life. We were staying at my grandmother's house. My mother, my grandmother, and my Uncle Heshke (my mother's older brother) were on a balcony overlooking a courtyard. Suddenly there was a commotion in the courtyard. A Lithuanian red-haired plainclothes policeman in a blue suit motioned for my uncle to come down. We never saw Uncle Heshke again. I think that this memory is incredibly significant because it stands for and represents all the important men in my life that have disappeared.

As I mentioned earlier, in those early years my mother was never around and when she was, she always seemed harsh and angry. The fact that she lost a husband, along with the demise of the family business, meant a significant loss of status that was particularly important for her self-esteem. My mother's anger was balanced by my grandmother's softness and pliability. My mother complained frequently about being burdened by the presence of a child. She regretted getting pregnant and on numerous occasions tried to abort the pregnancy, fortunately with little success. She did this by jumping downstairs and making herself vomit. She would tell me these things when she disapproved of my behavior. Maybe my stubborn nature stems partly from the fact that as hard as she tried, she could not extrude me from her body. At the same time, she would go to great lengths to reassure me that once I was born, she was glad. Sometimes I believed her, but just as often I did not.

As the Germans set up the Ghetto, they tried to squeeze all the Jews in Wilno into one small and old part of the city with narrow cobblestone streets. Fortunately, my grandparents' house and their business on 16 Rudnicka Street were just inside the border of the Ghetto close to the main gate. All of a sudden, there were all these strangers in our house and my mother, my grandmother, and I possessed the master bedroom, a luxury at the time. I remember walking through other parts of the house gingerly, to avoid stepping on people sleeping.

Gradually the number of people in the house diminished as people were removed from the Ghetto. In the meantime, I connected with other children that lived in other houses in the courtyard; I recall playing "war" and "hide and seek." When it rained, we would collect rainwater in buckets, which was used to wash clothing. However, I remember feeling restricted in our activities because of the constant fear that something bad was about to happen.

While I was not totally aware of what was transpiring, I did realize that people were disappearing—not a positive development even if it resulted in more space becoming available. The Germans would suddenly swoop down, night or day, and forcibly remove people from the streets and homes. These events were called "akcies" or actions. People were loaded into waiting trucks and we were told that they were being taken to labor camps. This implied that they were coming back. However, we soon realized that they were taken to destinations unknown and that they were not returning. Some people in their naiveté wanted to believe that people were going to labor camps; however, even they soon realized that people were being shipped somewhere from which they were not coming back. As a result, hiding became a commonplace activity when it was realized that the Germans were coming. We were preoccupied with finding new and more obscure and creative hiding places.

Once, we hid in the attic of my grandparents' house. There were many people; it was crowded, hot, and uncomfortable. There was no water or food, just a dish of rancid butter that was passed around from person to person. At first there was a sense that we were all in this together but after a while tempers were frayed and there were arguments. The stress of having to hide, and the fear of being caught and removed, were ever-present and anxiety-provoking.

Another time when we were hiding in a crowded basement, we were joined by a couple and a baby. The baby started to cry, and we could hear the Germans outside. If the baby did not stop crying, we would be discovered and that would be the end. Finally, someone suggested stuffing a rag in the baby's mouth to keep it quiet. Fortunately, it never came to that as the Germans left and we survived.

I remember looking out the window from my grandparents' house and observing several men being loaded into a truck. I recognized one of the men because his family stayed in our house. He was waving goodbye to his family as the truck was pulling away from the main gate.

What I did not understand nor appreciate at the time was that my grandparents' house was in a perfect location. It was on a corner where two large streets intersected, making it well-placed to see people going in and out of the enclosure. Since the enclosure was next to the main gate it was an excellent viewing area. One could see the guards changing shifts and their interactions. By their uniforms we could figure out how many were German, how many were Lithuanian, and how many were other nationalities. We realized that as the war progressed the number of German soldiers diminished while there were more guards that were German allies. We assumed that this shift in numbers was related to the German troops being sent to the front. Since the biggest portion of the house faced away from the Ghetto, we also had an unfettered view of what was happening outside. Half a block away there was a large handsome Catholic church, which attracted many worshippers, as Poland was primarily Catholic. No German soldiers attended church and as the war progressed there were fewer and fewer worshippers. We were also in a position to count ambulances since a large hospital was not far from the Ghetto. The more ambulances we saw going back and forth, especially in the winter, the more we assumed it to be a sign that Germany was losing the war. It was these kinds of observations—whether accurate or not—that fueled our optimism and hopes for the approaching liberation.

If part of our character structure is often shaped and molded by traumatic events from our childhood then this would partly explain my tendency to be quiet, somewhat secretive, and one to avoid attracting attention. While the dangers had dissipated many years ago the need to keep quiet and remain quiet and to stay in the background never left me. Being quiet means survival and is something that I have known and understood all my life. Ever since I was young, becoming quiet has been a safety mechanism for dealing with many difficult situations. However, being quiet is a double-edged sword. The dilemma is that one survives danger because quietness becomes a safety valve, but one also avoids potentially good situations because it takes time and is difficult for others to get to know you. On numerous occasions I have been told that people were turned off by my aloofness but were then pleasantly surprised when they got to know me better.

These incidents are some of my earliest memories of the occupation. I attribute meaning and significance to these events in determining who I was and who I became. I am also aware that our knowledge about how and why people are the way they are is limited. There are just too many variables shaping one's character. I feel somewhat entitled to attribute meaning to these horrific events and their impact on my psyche. However, before I become too glib in attributing causality to random events and occurrences, let's not lose sight of the fact that these incidents happened and the events occurred within a matrix of constant fear and terror.

3

LIFE IN THE GHETTO

(1941-1943)

THE WILNO GHETTO WAS CREATED in 1941 and liquidated in September 1943. The reason I know this latter date is because my mother and I escaped from the Ghetto the night before it was destroyed. It was one of numerous coincidences that contributed to our survival. The Ghetto had a population of between forty thousand and sixty thousand people. The only ghettos that were larger were the ones in Warsaw and Lodz.[4] The Jewish population of Wilno was between sixty thousand and eighty thousand people. After the war there were between one thousand and 1,300 Jewish survivors.

The Ghetto became a self-contained entity closed off by brick walls and barbed wire. That did not mean that individuals or even small groups

---

4   The Warsaw Ghetto was created in October of 1940 and liquidated in May of 1943. The city had a population of 672,000, including 270,000 Jews. It was the biggest of all the ghettos and the most resistant to extermination because of the uprising. The Lodz Ghetto was the second largest ghetto. It had a population of 163,000 of which 900 survived. It became a major industrial center because it produced useful military supplies. Because of its usefulness, the Lodz Ghetto was the last one to be liquidated, in August of 1944.

could not get out of the Ghetto—if they resorted to bribery or other creative means. Each day, there were work parties that went into the city proper. Several people managed to escape en route but later that changed. A number of the Lithuanian and Polish guards could be bribed with money and other favors. As a last resort there were the sewers. The odds of escaping the Ghetto were in your favor if you knew and/or maintained contact with Christian families in the city. Unfortunately, even those connections did not always work out because frequently, those families would betray potential escapees in exchange for rewards from the police. My mother had numerous connections in the city, so escaping from the Ghetto was not a major concern given that some of her trips involved trading and other basics such as food and medications.

The Judenrat (Jewish Council) was responsible for the administration of the Ghetto. There was also a Ghetto police whose job it was to maintain order and help the Germans round up people for deportation. I think that those that volunteered to be Ghetto police did so because they assumed that they would not be exterminated. Occasionally, the Ghetto police were beaten and even killed because their actions and activities were viewed as a betrayal. Jews killing Jews was something that the Germans could have cared less about. The general impression was that these individuals were from the lower stratum of the city's Jewish population, the so-called toughs. The leader of the Ghetto was a man named Jacob Gans. He must have been guided by some kind of mystical knowledge or magical fantasy that if he acceded to German demands on a regular basis, he would be able to save people. When he realized that this was not the case when the Germans made larger and larger demands for more people to be deported, he committed suicide.

The Germans were smart enough to realize that if they were able to help normalize life in the Ghetto, there would be much less resistance to the coming liquidation.

The Ghetto had excellent medical facilities, which predated the German occupation. Consequently, there were no major disease epidemics compared to other ghettos.

There were numerous cultural events such as original plays, lectures, and concerts. I remember attending plays with my grandmother and mother. There was a play that I went to see with my mother several times, but I do not recall its name. My mother knew the lead actress from her school days; we went backstage so my mother could say hello. I guess we did it because it made her feel important. I am sure that seeing plays made me feel good, especially given that such moments were few and far between. I remember certain original songs that we would hum and sing, including "Never Say That This Is the Final Path" and "My Name Is Sralik; I Am a Lad from the Ghetto." The lyrics of the latter song were about the fact that even though things are bad, we can still manage to jump, dance, and sing. I suppose that anything to make one feel good— and even hopeful—for a brief moment was important.

I think that people in the Ghetto made a concentrated effort to maintain a sense of normality under abnormal circumstances. Just how effective their efforts were is impossible to determine but the effort itself is both meaningful and deceptive because we were all waiting to die.

Most of the people we lived with were removed or found other places to live. Once again, the always unanswered question was, what happened to these people? The question was always met with a silent response.

However, there was one person who remained with us the entire time, including in hiding: Moshe. He was a heavyset man who was in his forties. He was alone and came from someplace in Poland. It was a mutually beneficial arrangement. We needed a male presence and he needed a family. Moshe was quiet and had a sad look on his face, but then everybody in the Ghetto looked sad. He was instrumental in our survival. He and my mother never got along—she would make snide comments about his lack of education and that he was secretive and did not reveal anything about himself. He sensed her arrogance, but I liked him because he was nice to me—maybe I reminded him of someone in his family that he lost. We assumed that most people that were herded into the Wilno Ghetto came from smaller towns whose ghettos were already liquidated. He probably lost his family but never said anything, at least to me.

I have little doubt that the main reason that I survived the Ghetto experience relatively unscathed emotionally was the love and protection of my grandmother. I would miss her more than anyone that I was ever close with. She shielded me and protected me from all the terrible things we were experiencing. It was like she enveloped me with her love so that nothing could harm me. She was always there no matter what the conditions or circumstances were. I can always recall her sad face, but I cannot remember her smile. But then how could she smile after experiencing so many losses?

Given the close and intimate protection of my grandmother and the distant presence of my mother, I felt relatively safe during those years in the Ghetto. However, I became aware of loss early on since it was a constant presence. I would get to know people and then suddenly they were gone. When I would ask where they were, all that I got were blank looks and an all-encompassing silence. I learned relatively early that children are not supposed to mention or ask about painful issues.

While I was not privy to the conversations and dealings of the adults around me, I got the sense that something was being planned and I did not dare ask what it was. I was sure that my questions would not be answered so I learned to keep quiet and to pretend that I was oblivious, even though that was not the case at all.

I observed, I noticed, and on some level I understood what was happening all around me. I observed and even understood that these are useful qualities, but to act oblivious is sometimes useful for survival. I recognized rumblings having to do with leaving and escaping the Ghetto. By this time German pronouncements about labor camps were meaningless because nobody who left ever came back. There were rumors of concentration camps where people were gassed. Not far from Wilno was a place called Ponar (Ponari in Polish) where people were killed and their bodies were covered with soil and lime. I am assuming that a large portion of the Ghetto population is buried in Ponar. Although I have never gone back to Wilno, I have heard that a major monument has been erected in the area.

There was black bunting on the trees when the Russians defeated the Germans at Stalingrad. There were recurrent rumors that the Germans were losing the war and there was the awareness that we would be killed or sent to concentration camps before the Russians could liberate us. There were rumors from work parties that people escaped into the forests to become and to join the partisans. The forests in Poland and Belarus were frequently where people went when they escaped the Ghetto. While the surrounding forests were relatively safe havens of survival, we also heard that the Polish and Lithuanian populations were of little assistance to the escapees. We knew that there was a significant likelihood that Jews would be turned over for a significant reward.

Each time the Germans realized that people escaped from work parties, they would kill a certain number of people in retaliation. We heard that there were weapons in the Ghetto for a possible confrontation but ultimately the decision was made to fight from the forests instead. Because the Germans were being shipped to the Russian Front, the Poles and the Lithuanians became our primary executioners. There was no doubt that the Poles and the Lithuanians took to their tasks with glee. After the war, the Poles in particular went to great lengths to deny participation in the killings and made the point that they were also victims and were being killed by the Germans and later by the Russians. This excuse was only valid if they chose to rebel against the occupiers, which they did not.

I finally understood that my mother's frantic activity and occasional disappearances had something to do with escaping the Ghetto. In conjunction with other people, my mother was setting up a hiding place outside of the city. While I have been critical of my mother 's mothering and her relationship with my grandmother, I was equally cognizant of her many strengths and the resilience of her character. She was very resourceful as she had ample funds at her disposal that she had buried so she could recover them after the liberation. These funds were mostly Russian gold coins considered safe and valuable.

Moshe, who lived with us for two years, escaped the Ghetto by bribing the guards. He was out there setting up the place where we were going to hide with several other people. What made it all possible was my mother's drive, toughness, and finances.

How this all came together, including organization and the various people involved, was never explained. All I knew was that there was a place waiting somewhere out there and at the proper time we would walk out the front gate. On a couple of occasions, the plans were changed because the guards changed; on another night it was not dark enough—it had to be pitch-black for us to leave. My mother maintained contact with a number of people who were equally committed to escaping. However, who and how the plan came together was never explicit since there was more than one person in charge of this project. Due to limited space and resources, the whole undertaking had to be completely secret; if word got out that an escape was planned more people would want to join. There was also the question of who could be trusted since there were people in the Ghetto who cooperated with the Germans. There was ample evidence that they would not hesitate to pass on the information.

The prearranged day for the escape finally arrived. All that I remember is that it was cold and dark. I was dressed in several layers of clothing, and there was a limit as to how much stuff we could carry.

My grandmother and I stood in the courtyard next to the gate while my mother negotiated with the guards about the money they were getting. As my mother was walking back, I realized that my grandmother was not coming with us and that we were leaving her behind. As I was saying goodbye to her I asked if I would ever see her again and she said that she did not know. All I remember is the next moment, my mother grabbed me by the hand and we hurriedly walked out the gate. It seemed that she almost pulled my arm out of its socket.

The question of why we left my grandmother behind is something that has haunted me most of my life. The simple way of looking at it is that for everyone who survives someone else must pay the price—I lived and my grandmother died. That doesn't answer the basic question about the choices that people have to make, but such choices were a part of the Holocaust equation. I missed my grandmother and asked my mother about it. Her response was a vague dismissive comment that I wouldn't understand. My mother was never good at confronting emotionally charged issues such as what my father was like and why my grandmother was left behind. Maybe it was a practical decision: my grandmother would be too much of a burden because of her age. Maybe the guards would allow only two people to leave so my mother had to make a painful choice. It was also possible that my grandmother refused to leave and chose to remain where things were familiar rather than take a chance on the unknown. When I was little, I felt that it was my fault that she died and my mother chose to save me instead. My mother was excellent at reinforcing that belief. Whenever she was unhappy with me about something, she would let me know that she wished she had left me behind instead of my grandmother. It was obviously her own guilt, which she displaced onto me. Nevertheless, as much as I would try to rationalize her decision, the guilt was never distant.

Many years after these events occurred—after I was married and had a family, and after I spent years in analysis—my mother was visiting us. She had gotten upset with me about something I did or most likely did not do, and then reminded me that she chose to save me and leave my grandmother behind. I told her that one of the reasons she made that choice is that my grandmother favored her brother Hatchie over her. My mother was so shocked and taken aback by my interpretation that she turned pale as a ghost and her lower lip trembled, but nothing emerged from her mouth. She never made that guilt-provoking comment again.

4

HIDING

(1943-1944)

AS WE EXITED THE GHETTO, I was crying so hard that I couldn't see—the experience became one big blur. My mother was clutching my hand as I was stumbling next to her. I felt like I was being dragged. We crossed Mickiewicza, a major boulevard, and then walked up the stairs and into an apartment. I asked my mother where we were going but got no response. As it turned out we were spending the night in the home of a Polish couple that used to work for my parents. I found out that these people were storing some of my parents' valuables for safekeeping until the liberation. If we did not make it or did not survive, all these belongings would remain with this family. We experienced a sense of relief and liberation in leaving the Ghetto, but little did we know that our prison-like experience was just beginning.

We woke up the next morning to a gloomy rainy day. The sky was overcast as thick dark clouds rolled in over the city. The weather was a

29

good thing, as my mother and I would be less likely to be noticed. After we ate the gentleman told us that the Ghetto was surrounded by German troops, meaning it was being liquidated. I did not fully comprehend that all the residents of the Ghetto were being sent to concentration camps. I still nurtured the faint hope that my grandmother would survive and that I would see her again. I entertained that fantasy for a long time until it finally hit me that she was all alone with the knowledge that she would soon die.

We then prepared to trek across the city to our prepared hiding place. My mother had a dark complexion and dark curly hair, so she wrapped a thick scarf around her head to cover most of her features. I was fair-skinned and had blond hair, so my head was left uncovered, even though it was cold. Such a precaution was essential since we were close to the Ghetto. There was at least one other time that my being fair-skinned with blond hair was an asset that may have contributed to our survival.

To get away from the vicinity of the Ghetto as quickly as possible my mother hailed a horse-drawn carriage to take us away from the city. I could tell that it was far from the city because the house that we entered was next to the railroad yards and was situated in the middle of nowhere, away from the prying eyes of neighbors. We entered a small, undistinguished looking cottage, which was inhabited by an older woman with two unmarried daughters. The house had all sorts of religious icons and crosses on the walls, which to me was both strange and fascinating. This reaction coincided with a similar experience years later when I had surgery at a Catholic Hospital—above my bed loomed an image of Christ (more on this later). I guess I should not complain since I survived both situations. Being exposed to all these non-Jewish religious items thrust at me for the first time in my life made me extremely uncomfortable. I felt that I was being disloyal to the one and only Jewish deity.

The old woman who was going to hide us was short and squat; she had sharp, witch-like features and a deformed spine. One of her daughters had reddish hair with an angry pinched face while her other daughter was nondescript. My mother and the old woman engaged in a lengthy discussion that probably dealt with the payment for hiding us. We then walked a couple hundred yards to a large tool shed on a hillock. We entered the shed through large doors with huge windows that looked out to the railroad yards. There were wooden counters around the walls of the shed and beneath one of the counters there was a trap door that went down a ladder into a cellar that contained eighteen other people. This hiding place was to be our home for the next eleven months until the liberation by the Russian army. The whole set-up seemed rickety and primitive, but we had no choice. The cellar seemed solid by comparison to the shed above.

Initially, the people we joined in the cellar did not appear distinctive, which was probably a function of the darkness and my anxiety. I then noticed a blond-haired boy who was a couple years older than I, Lolek, who was there with his parents. There was an attractive young woman named Rivka, probably in her twenties and alone. Our friend Moshe who stayed in our house in the Ghetto was there. His was a comforting, familiar face.

How these various individuals were chosen was a mystery since they were not related to one another, nor did they seem to have any prior connections. I could only speculate that the choices were based on money. My mother and I were the last ones to arrive. How long the selection process lasted was also a mystery, but I knew that some people were admitted because they threatened to reveal the group's existence to the Ghetto police otherwise.

Harmony was nonexistent; there were frequent fights, no doubt about space and money. While in theory we should have become one big happy cooperative family, this never became a reality until the very end, when everyone's survival was at stake. Until that desperate moment we existed in a constant state of tension and fear. Emotions ran high and tempers flared. There was fear about what was happening outside, especially when it came to trusting the three women. No one felt comfortable putting our faith in the hands of these three unknown individuals. We had no idea what they were thinking, and wondered if they would betray us. Because they were paid in advance, we were totally at their mercy. I think that we also experienced fear of each other, as tempers were short and we were strangers thrown together in a confined space.

How this place was set up ahead of time and who was involved in building it was never discussed. How this Polish family was found was not known. They took a large risk in making this commitment to hide us from the Nazis; one could label them as "righteous gentiles" except they got a lot of money for doing this. At the end they tried to betray us, but it was too late. Regardless, they took a big risk because if they were discovered, they would have been shot for harboring Jews. For that alone we should have appreciated what they did, but that was lost in the drama of the liberation.

My mother was not the most trusting person, so I assumed that she knew some of the people we were staying with (besides Moshe) and must have trusted them. They managed to escape from the Ghetto at various times and in different groups, so I came to learn each one's story. I assumed Moshe must have been involved in the construction of the place. I assume that my mother made use of her unlimited financial resources by paying for him because he had no money.

Seeing our hiding place for the first time must have made a profound impression on me. I guess you could call it a basement, but to me it looked like a big cavern that housed twenty bodies of various shapes and sizes. The characteristic of the place that has stayed with me all these years is the darkness. There was no electricity, we had candles that were hardly used, and the walls were brick and very thick. The only light was a brick that was removed from the wall, which let in the daylight. However, when it was a dark or a gloomy day there was no light and we lived in semi-darkness. Whether by chance or design, I think it is significant that the missing brick was from the eastern wall. The Russian armies that liberated us came from the east.

I was always conscious of which incidents from my time in the Ghetto left permanent marks on my personality. Avoiding darkness at all costs was a significant preoccupation in my life. I favor lots of lights. Whether it is in my office or at home, I prefer many lamps and high-powered light bulbs. This puts me in direct conflict with those committed to saving money by dimming lights to use less electricity.

The beds were lined up along the walls; most of the people had few belongings, as there was little room. The place was clean and well maintained as people tried to cooperate on a day-to-day basis, which was difficult because we were in such close proximity. Most of the time we stayed downstairs and only in the evening would we venture into the shed above, two or three people at a time. This was essential in order to keep it quiet and not call attention to the shed but also to enjoy the little freedom that was allotted us. The three women who took care of us made sure that we stayed within the proscribed boundaries.

We had a strange and hostile dependent relationship with our three caretakers. They brought us food twice a day in large pails and buckets while removing waste products. The two daughters brought us our meals, and we never saw the old lady except at the very end. The food consisted of soups, bread, vegetables, and fruits. We did not observe dietary laws and the food was adequate, evidenced by the fact that we did not starve.

I saw the women briefly as there were minimal verbal interactions. They were brief and grim in their manner and always looked annoyed. Once, one of the men asked what was going on with the war. Instead of answering, they stared at us blankly and walked away. We were unable to tell if their response was due to a lack of understanding or just hostility. From that moment we avoided all conversation with them except to say thank you. On two occasions they scared us by banging on the shed's doors when we got into loud discussions in the evening.

I do not remember some of the people, even though we were thrown together for almost a year. However, I can recall the individuals that had an impact on me. The person I remember the most was a gentleman in his fifties whose last name was Yablonsky. He may have been a rabbi (or maybe became one later) as my mother visited him in Israel many years after the war. He was a great storyteller and so I spent a lot of time with him partly because we both experienced physical problems, me with my sensitive stomach while he complained of arthritic pains. I have clear memories of lying on the bunk next to his and being enthralled by stories about the Tales of the Arabian Nights, Sinbad the Sailor, and Princess

Scheherazade. He was very kind and would tell my mother what a great memory I had and that someday I would be a good student. This made her proud. All the other people looked up to him because of his wisdom; people came to him to settle disputes. Such responsibilities kept him busy, and everyone listened to him and abided by his decisions. His presence was a unifying force. He was the moral compass of the group and the final arbiter of all disagreements.

Another person that stood out in my mind was Rivka. She was personable, outgoing, and most importantly, she spoke German fluently. Every Jew who knows Yiddish thinks that he can speak German. That is inaccurate—Yiddish is a combination of German, Hebrew, Polish, Russian, and who knows what else. Rivka learned German in school and spoke it flawlessly. She was instrumental in our survival because of her language skills. After the war, my mother kept in touch with her and visited her in London. I guess these people with whom we had contentious relationships while hiding were perhaps more meaningful and important than we realized. My mother and I were curious about what happened to them and how they were doing. Most of the people that were with us in hiding disappeared immediately after the war and we did not make any effort to track them down except for Mr. Yablonsky and Rivka.

Lolek was the only other youngster among us; he was twelve (I was eight). For some reason he and I never connected although he was always pleasant. Maybe the age difference was too large. I ran into him after the liberation and he introduced me to his friends as someone that he survived with. That made me feel good and maybe I looked up to him as the older brother I never had. The only other people that I remember are a family by the name of Epstein consisting of a couple in their forties with an adolescent boy and girl. I did not care for Mr. Epstein because he acted like a know-it-all and was always engaged in arguments with everyone. I always wondered why I expended so little effort in getting to know everyone who was there as they treated me well. The only explanation that makes some sense is that because most of the people seemed in conflict with one another it scared me and kept me from getting close to them.

Thinking back, I could not help but wonder what we did all the time and how we passed the days. Our minimal reading material was in Polish; we did not have games or any other materials that could be used to occupy all this free time. Perhaps this was one of the reasons why there were so many arguments: there were no outlets to discharge excess emotional energy. Boredom and anxiety were a constant presence.

When there are a number of people under stress in an enclosed space for a long time, there is bound to be bickering. The arguments were frequent and loud. Once, in the midst of a heated argument, there was a sudden loud banging on the shed doors. It was one of the gentile women who must have overheard us and tried to impress on us to stop. While the intent was appropriate, she could have done it in a way that didn't scare us so much. The arguments did not decrease in frequency, but they diminished in intensity. I must have become used to the bickering because I am unable to recall any of the content that was being argued. My assumption is that it had something to do with limited space because of the tight quarters, but it may have also been related to the pecking order of the group.

As mentioned earlier, in the evenings we would open the trap door and climb up into the shed in small groups on a rotating basis. We looked forward to these upper-level excursions as it gave us a chance to experience the outer world without stepping outside. I have vague memories of looking at the sky and the stars. There were also trains going back and forth in the railroad yards. I kept hearing the same stories over and over again, which made me assume that we were all feeling pretty bored. There were numerous stories about what life was like before the war. My mother was afforded some deference because of her wealth and status before the war.

One evening, when we were in the shed, someone dropped something accidentally, making a loud noise. A guard patrolling the railroad yards heard it and looked in our direction. We froze, and it seemed that he was staring right at us even though he was several hundred yards away. We were fearful that he would come to investigate, but instead he continued on his rounds. We breathed a sigh of relief.

Even though the time dragged on, spring turned into summer and we had an inkling that there were changes in the air unrelated to the change of seasons. The railroad yards became busier with more traffic at night and we could count the trains carrying personnel and supplies from west to east. We could also see an increase in fortifications such as antiaircraft batteries, camouflage, and lots of barbed wire. Soon we were able to figure out the reason for this heightened activity.

One night during all this commotion we heard numerous airplanes overhead, as well as sirens, searchlights, and the explosion of bombs. We assumed correctly that these were Russian planes and we were joyful that the war was coming closer. Were we on the threshold of liberation? Our initial excitement subsided when a bomb exploded within our line of sight. A large piece of the bomb's casing fell against the outside wall of the shed and lodged beneath one of the windows. That could have easily decimated a portion of our hiding place. When this hiding place was chosen, we did not fully appreciate that railroad yards would become an appealing and inviting target for enemy bombs. Initially, the air raids were only at night—after a while they increased in frequency and intensity and then they occurred in broad daylight. Sleeping became more difficult because people were anxious about being bombed and would often stay up at night to keep track of what was going on.

There was a great deal of activity in our area with an increased massing of troops in the railroad yards and an increase in fortifications.

All three of the gentile women showed up one day to discuss future plans and changes in routine. This was only the second time during our stay that I observed the older woman. She looked angry and to me, she seemed hideous. It was evident that the war zone was moving closer, but we had no idea just how this change would affect us. The first thing that she demanded was that from now on we had to remain in the cellar all the time—since there were many more eyes around us, we needed to avoid being detected or seen. No more visits to the shed at night. The three women would remain in their house, which meant that there would be less frequent visits, which implied less food. They demanded that we ration the food from now on. Even in the cellar we were expected to remain quiet and whisper to one another. They were aware of our tendency to argue—such activities were out of the question. When we dared to ask what was going on, we got no response except for the usual silence.

They became much more cognizant of the possibility of being discovered and the implication of our presence. I suppose that they could have always pleaded ignorance about our presence on their property. They could be ignorant when it came to one or two people being there, but how could you explain twenty people hiding on their property without their awareness? Any possible explanation would be an untenable excuse.

As the days of increased confinement wore on, we became more tense and spent every second peering out of our little bricked window for telltale signs of what was going on outside. We created all sorts of fantasies and fanciful scenarios about the external activities. We were hoping for a quick German surrender and the appearance of Russian troops. Instead, what occurred was the polar opposite of what we hoped and wished for. It was something that we were totally unprepared for.

As the bombings diminished, we became aware of artillery fire, which meant that the war zone was drawing closer and we were in the middle of it. We kept track of the explosions and their intensity, but our conclusions were pure guesswork. We lost complete contact with the three women, becoming totally isolated from the outside world and without food or water.

We were aware of a marked increase in the frantic activity above us and heard much talking and the barking of orders in German. Instead of our wishes for a German surrender, it became evident that our shed had become the focus of another Stalingrad-like battle. We had a sense of being trapped between the Germans and the Russians. I had no inkling at the time that this was going to become the most horrendous week of my life.

5

LIBERATION

(1945)

AFTER BEING COOPED UP FOR long stretches of time with limited access to the outside world we became extremely attuned to what was transpiring outside the cellar. In fact, this was how we assessed the military situation that we were in the midst of. The Russians were in a village a couple hundred yards away; we knew this because we could see the red flag. The Russians were very fond of their artillery, so they used that instead of infantry to attack the Germans directly.

The Germans were in a great position defensively as our cellar and shed were on a small hill with excellent visual command of the area. They had either one or two machine guns, which kept the Russians at bay by spraying the area intermittently. The staccato machine gun noise became a familiar sound. There emerged a military stalemate between the Russian artillery and the German machine guns. The Russians were hoping that their superior artillery could knock out the German machine guns and then their liberation of the area would involve minimal warfare. The problem with that plan was that we were caught in the middle of the two armies without food or water. This standoff lasted four days. Our impressions of what was going on militarily were surprisingly accurate, as our liberators later informed us. However, having a sense of what was happening did not make us any less anxious.

We lost complete contact with the three women; it was as if they disappeared from the face of the earth. Since it was the middle of summer it was extremely hot, and we became desperate. Two of our group drank their own urine. I licked the dew from the walls in the morning. The tension, the thirst, and the hunger were just too much. We could tolerate the hunger, but the thirst was torturous. All the stresses combined were just too much: the Germans above us, our uncertain fate, and liberation so close yet so far. On the third day of our confinement, Mr. Epstein, his teenage son, and our friend Moshe lifted the trap door and ran out of the cellar without saying a word. They did not say anything—they just did it. Where they planned to go and what they were planning to accomplish was not clear—this was a desperate suicidal act. After they left, we waited for the Germans to come down. However, nothing happened except the constant rattling of the machine guns.

We deliberated what to do and how long we could tolerate such conditions. There were suggestions that we should just run out into the open and take our chances. Maybe we should tell them who we are and hope that they would be merciful and let us live. If we all ran out and scattered in different directions, it was likely that at least some of us would survive.

On the afternoon of the fourth day the thing we dreaded most finally occurred. The trap door opened very slowly, and the head of a helmeted German soldier peered into our hiding place. He came down the ladder, followed by a second and then a third soldier. They looked around with a certain amusement. What they saw was a bunch of women and two blond-haired boys. The five men were out of sight, hidden behind clothing and blankets under the beds.

Rivka, our German-speaking savior, sprang into action. She told them in flawless German that we were Poles and were hiding from the Russians. We heard that the Russian soldiers are cruel; that they rape women and kill innocent women and children. All the Germans could see were terrified women and children while the five men remained invisible under the beds. She told them that we were hungry and thirsty after hiding from the Russians for four days. None of Rivka's story was planned; it was a spontaneous narrative that the Germans believed.

To this day I will never understand why they believed us. They made no connection between us and the three men that ran out the day before. Maybe Rivka was a great actress; maybe we looked too frightened and too haggard to be a threat. These were frontline troops who were probably too preoccupied with their own survival in the midst of fighting a war. They could not possibly be curious about who we were and why we were there. So, for the next three days we coexisted with the Wehrmacht. They treated us well; gave us water, a little food—one of the soldiers gave me a piece of chocolate. They never looked for nor did they discover the men; we smuggled them food and water. I guess one becomes philosophical at such times with the possibility that some higher power was watching over us, as the Germans never considered checking the place for the presence of others.

For three days, we shared our space with the enemy, who could turn on us at any minute and kill us. When people are involved in a war every stranger is a potential enemy that needs to be eliminated. In the heat of battle everything is possible as soldiers are not interested in making fine distinctions between who is a friend and who is an enemy. The fear and the terror that consumed us during those three days were beyond comprehension. We felt that we were under the gun the whole time with no avenue for escape.

It became obvious that our hiding place had become a primary fortification against the onrushing Red Army. By the second day the Germans built a trench through the cellar to the back of the shed, where they set up a command post. There was a table with a map, telephones, and all sorts of wires. Constant orders were going back and forth, some of which we understood. There was an invisible wall between them and us as they went about the business of war while all that we cared about was the business of survival. It was essential for us to remember to talk in Polish among ourselves, which was not easy and occasionally forgotten. Rivka became like a veritable policewoman and our conscience to make sure that we were quiet, whispered only in Polish, and that Lolek and myself were prominently displayed.

There was a major incident during the second day of our coexistence. The Germans had dug into their positions solidly while the Russian artillery shelling intensified. Suddenly, a Russian artillery shell made a direct hit on the east wall of our cellar and it seemed as if everything exploded. The wall started to crumble, bricks were flying all over; there was dust, chaos, and the strong smell of gunpowder. People were screaming and a woman was sobbing in Yiddish that she was being buried alive. Other women removed the bricks and she was fine: someone put their hand over her mouth to keep her quiet. She was calmed down temporarily.

In my panic to get away from the chaos and into a place of safety, I ran into the German command post. All that stayed in my mind was the smell of the exploding shell and the realization that on one side our cellar and shed were completely exposed. The German soldiers shoed me back into the cellar as they were yelling "raus, raus," which means "get out." The next thing that I remembered was someone grabbing me by the shoulder and pulling me back into the cellar. In some miraculous way, except for a few minor scratches, the explosion injured no one. The older woman continued to scream and cry in Yiddish and once again someone covered her mouth. After the explosion, one-half of our hiding place was destroyed. There was no place to hide from the elements or the constant shooting.

Some of the men from our group were terrified of being buried alive so we repositioned them while the soldiers were too busy to notice. The soldiers congregated in the command post pouring over their maps while we hoped they were planning to retreat. While this was going on, they gave us some crackers and water. It was obvious that they had more important things on their minds than us. As far as they were concerned, we did not exist.

With our cellar wall blown away we saw the red flag fluttering majestically in the breeze; it was our beacon to freedom. We were also aware of much more activity in the flag area, which meant that the Russian troops could be massing for a frontal assault on the German positions. It seemed that the Nazi machine guns were not chattering as frequently.

We were in a constant state of dread mixed with excitement, the result of having no idea what was coming next. We sat and lay on the floor like statues, not moving. Now, we were wide-open targets, afraid of the Russian artillery. Someone suggested that we wave a piece of red cloth, but it was decided that was too dangerous. We sat there rooted to our spots waiting for the next explosion—it never came.

By the third night it became evident that the Germans were getting ready to retreat. It was getting quieter and looked like they were collecting their equipment, disconnecting the phone cables, and folding the maps. We heard snippets of conversation but there were fewer voices and some strange sounds. A German officer came to talk to Rivka. He told her that they were leaving and going back to the city to continue the battle. They suggested that we come along, as the Russians are wild animals that rape women and kill children. For our safety we should retreat with them, otherwise he could not guarantee our fate. She thanked him for his concern and said that she needed to consult with the rest of the group to make it look like we were debating what to do. We had no intention of retreating with the Germans: so far, we had been fortunate. She went back and told him that the children were sick from the lack of food and water and were too weak to go anywhere. The hidden issue was the men under the beds and what would happen to them if we left. The soldier wished us luck when Rivka told him that we would take our chances and remain where we were. He said he could not do any more for us, said goodbye, and left.

The rest of that night was probably one of the longest nights of our lives as we sat and waited. We still had no idea about what was going on around us. We heard women's voices and thought the three Polish women would betray us to the Germans who, in turn, would blow us up or just decide to shoot us. Then there was the question of what had happened to the three men that ran out. Where were they? Would they tell the Germans about us? For the entire night, we sat in total silence and darkness not knowing what was going to happen. It seemed like any minute something bad could occur. The night was eerily quiet.

At dawn it began to rain, at first heavy, then settling into a light drizzle. Still, we refused to move—everything around us was quiet while the explosions moved further and further away. We sat in what was left of our shelter, completely exposed.

The silence was broken when we suddenly heard these Russian words that I will never forget: "Gde Commandir nashey roti?" "Where is the commander of our squad?" We looked at each other and did not know what to do. We were about to respond when someone said it could be the Germans trying to trick us; if we respond, they will shoot us. We just sat there on our pile of rubble, as one after another Russian soldier appeared. All of a sudden, we realized that we survived. We thanked them, embraced them, shook their hands, and cried. We kept saying "sposibo, sposibo," Russian for "thank you." We also kept saying "ivrei," Russian for "Jews." The Russians were friendly, but they looked at us quizzically because they could not figure out who we were and how we got there. Fortunately, two of the people in our group knew some Russian so they tried to explain our presence, but the soldier could not comprehend what they were being told. We started to worry that they would see us as spies or subversives. The war was still going on and during war you cannot trust anyone, especially when people are in a place where they do not belong. The Russian soldiers were skeptical because they knew that the Poles and Lithuanians cooperated with the Germans.

There was a certain beauty and irony in our liberation that was significant. The commanding officer of the troops that liberated us was a major and a Jew. He said that we were the first Jews that he encountered since the city of Smolensk in White Russia or Belarus, which was four hundred kilometers away. The beauty of this is that a Jew liberated us—to be freed from the Nazis by a Jew was the ultimate victory and does not get any better than that.

The officer kept marveling at how we survived since he aimed his artillery to fire point-blank at our shed and cellar. The Russians were puzzled about how we wound up in this seemingly forsaken place, how the Germans did not kill us, and how their artillery did not kill or even wound anyone of us.

In the film *Schindler's List* there is a poignant scene at the end in which the survivors are walking together in the empty countryside as if lost and confused. They have a glazed look on their faces as they walk directionless. A Russian soldier says to them, "Now that you are free, where will you go? You have no place to go."

This is how we were those first few days after the liberation: in a fog, confused, dazed, not believing that we were free. We had no purpose and had to stay put because fighting was raging in the city. The Germans, true to their promise, continued to fight till the bitter end.

The first step we took was to find the three men that ran out from our hiding place and then find the three Polish women that hid us. We found all six of them, dead. Moshe, the heavyset man who attached himself to us, could not run very far, so he was shot not far from the shed. The father and son were much further away from the shed; a hand grenade tore up their bodies. As one would expect the mother and daughter fell apart when they discovered what happened to the rest of their family. The mother kept wailing uncontrollably, "Why did you have to run out? I begged you to stay put but you wouldn't listen. You had a chance to survive but you threw it away."

We found the three Polish women close to their house; they were dead, naked, and covered by a metal sheet. All three were shot and lying next to one another. Maybe the Germans shot them and were getting ready to shoot us but ran out of time. Why were they naked? Were they raped? If they were, was it by the Germans or the Russians? Maybe that had something to do with the voices we heard that last night. It was one of those mysteries that would not make sense nor lend itself to a plausible explanation. There were no dead Russians that we could see in our vicinity. Either the Russians quickly removed their dead or there just weren't any in our immediate area. There were bodies of two Germans, but they were ignored as if they were not there. The Russians got some of the locals to remove the bodies of the three women while we buried our dead with plans to come back to give them a proper Jewish burial. That actually happened about a week after the liberation.

There were so many things about our survival that just did not make sense. So many negative and potentially destructive events and situations that we walked away from, unscathed. There were incidents that could have gone in either direction yet turned out positively, especially that last week. We did lose those three members of our group as a result of their impatience. I cried when I saw Moshe's body; I felt a fondness for him and would miss him.

Why were the Germans so oblivious to who we were and what we were there for? After all, our story just didn't add up. If we were so afraid of the Russians, then why did we stay behind? How could they not realize the men who ran out must have been related to us in some manner? The people forgetting and talking in Yiddish, which sounds a little like German. The list of coincidences and contradictions defies explanation and understanding.

How was it that there were all these contradictions that were ignored and not responded to? Was our survival explained by a bunch of coincidences that turned out in our favor almost all the time? Isn't that a rather simplistic explanation of a complicated set of events that came together in a positive way? Is it equally possible that we survived because of a miracle or a series of miracles that piggybacked on one another? Besides, just what is a miracle or what constitutes a miracle? This was not in any way a religious group that prayed in any significant manner. The events of the last night in the cellar just did not make sense. As much as I have tried to piece things together in a coherent narrative that is internally and externally consistent, it just does not seem to come together. So instead, I have to settle for something that I learned in my training many years ago—that there are so many things in this world that just do not make sense. To try and understand what transpired is a useless undertaking. I am assuming that each one of us that survived will make up their own story about the experience—in the long run, it is the best that we can hope for.

It was the summer of 1944 and even though I was only eight years old I knew that something was different and that something was starting to change inside of me. I knew that we survived some bad things, but my mother and I came out of it in decent shape. I started to think about the future: going to school, running around with other kids, riding bikes and reading books, which I had never done before. These thoughts kept coming back over and over, as they were a harbinger of things to come. It occurred to me to remember and to record all the terrible things that happened, what we had been through, and that we survived. As all these thoughts were swirling in my head, I knew then and there that this was not the end of anything at all but just the beginning.

6

THE AFTERMATH

(1944-1948)

MY MEMORIES FROM THE TIME after the liberation were not etched as sharply as those from the Ghetto and our hiding place. Maybe this is because these periods had so many powerful emotions attached to them while those that came after were less emotional. I do not remember exactly how long we hung out by our former hiding place; however, we were reluctant to leave because we were still attached to its sense of safety, plus there was ongoing fighting in the city. It made no sense to go anywhere or do anything. A week after the fighting we buried our dead; Mr. Yablonsky said a prayer and we put up a temporary marker out of respect. I recall some of us crying while the rest stared blankly. The Russians got some of the locals to take care of the bodies of the gentile women.

As the fighting moved farther west, people drifted back to the city. Some of our group of survivors left without even saying goodbye. Maybe there was so much pain attached to the recent events we shared that saying goodbye was just too uncomfortable. Maybe it was easier to drift away without acknowledging what we just experienced and how significant and important we became to one another. Perhaps we became too attached to everyone during those eleven months that getting away from such painful connections seemed like a good idea. I think we must have felt emptiness once the purpose for our existence together evaporated.

While in later years we sought out and spent time with a few other survivors, now we just wanted to get away. I have to give my mother credit in this regard because she actively sought out and connected with a couple of the people, specifically Rivka and Mr. Yablonsky. As I noted earlier, she kept in touch with them for a long time, especially Rivka, whom she loved and admired for her coolness under fire. Most of us agreed that if it were not for her quick thinking none of us would have survived.

Part of the time that we were there we continued to wonder about the events of our survival. So many events happened that could have gone in either direction yet turned out in our favor, especially that last week. Once the fog lifted from our psyche and the glaze disappeared from our eyes, my body reacted to the changes in a familiar fashion: I got sick. I developed diarrhea because I ate many things that I should not have eaten. The quality and quantity of the food was just too much and I paid the price. I was also severely sunburned. My skin was fair, and I was used to semi-darkness for almost a year, so I could not adapt to the scorching summer sun. I developed blisters all over my body along with a high fever. The Russian army medic prescribed something to take care of the blisters while he insisted that I stay in bed for several days. To finally be free to roam the railroad yards at will and then be forced to remain bedridden made me unhappy and angry with the medic and my mother, who took his advice.

In her usual manner my mother disappeared as soon as the city was safe. She was looking for survivors. Her efforts were not successful, however; finding things instead of people was her forte. Did she look for my father? If she did, where did she look? Not many people returned that were actually involved in the fighting. Did she look for my grandmother? Perhaps she asked some concentration camp survivors about her. If she did, she never told me and so seemingly accepted the verdict that everyone that meant something to her had died.

She dug up some more gold pieces and retrieved most of her belongings from the Polish couple. My mother was a very practical and resourceful person who kept track of everything that belonged to her and the family. However, she was also generous toward the people that helped her retrieve her belongings, so she left them some valuable items as a sign of her appreciation.

She located an abandoned apartment, large and barren-looking since we had no furniture. My mother found two distant relatives who retreated with the Russian army but had come back to Wilno. One decided to stay in the city and got a government job while the other relative disappeared.

It was still my fate to spend many hours alone while she roamed the city looking for things. Maybe she spent her time searching for family survivors, but if she did, she never said anything about it. She went back to my grandparents' house; it was empty and it looked like it had been ransacked. She also went back to the house where she and my father lived, but it was occupied by a Lithuanian couple. That was the only information I was able to get. I wanted to see my grandparents' house since I lived there but she did not think that was a good idea. I think that I was hopeful that my grandmother would suddenly appear to claim her house, but I knew that it was a ridiculous expectation. Nevertheless, it was one more reason to be angry with my mother, even if it was irrational.

The third week after the liberation we received an unpleasant surprise, which turned our lives upside down. We got awakened in the middle of the night by air raid sirens, searchlights, and bombs raining down on the city. The Germans decided to exact revenge for having lost recent battles. My mother and I ran down the street in our night clothes and hid in a bombed-out building. Someone told her that it was a safe place to stay during an air raid. There were bombs whistling overhead and we had good reason to be terrified once again. One never gets used to the sound of whistling bombs coming down since who knows which one will take your last breath. I always had a sinking feeling in my stomach until the whistling stopped and the bomb exploded. We were afraid to return to our apartment because of the possibility that there may have been Germans there; our fear of them was that pervasive. Two Russian soldiers were kind enough to escort us upstairs as they were joking about seeing Germans jumping out of airplanes. Even then we stayed up the rest of the night. The next day there were rumors that the Germans were coming back, and the bombing raid was a prelude to their return. I am sure it made the Lithuanians and the Poles happy as they awaited the Germans' return so that they could be free to kill the few Jewish survivors.

While I have always given my mother credit for her common sense, perseverance, resourcefulness, good judgment, and intensity about where we should go from here, this time her judgment failed. After asking numerous people what to do, she impulsively decided that we needed to leave the city and hide in the countryside because she was convinced the Germans were coming back. The fear of the Nazis was so strong and pervasive that even though the news from the war front was positive, she did not trust it. At the time, the decision to do this made sense. Nevertheless, it was totally driven by fear and a deep distrust of the idea that the Germans could possibly be beaten.

She tracked down a farm about twenty kilometers from Wilno that agreed to have us stay with them for a price. But the footnote to this deal was that if the Germans returned, the family would be obligated to shelter us. While the idea had some merit there was no way that we could hold them to such a commitment. They may go along with the idea or they would be the first ones to sell us out and plunder our few belongings. Once again, we were in a precarious position, at the mercy of people that we did not know and who most likely hated us.

We stayed there for four to five weeks and it turned out to be one of the more unpleasant periods of my life. As usual my mother was away most of the time. I found myself at the mercy of a couple of older Polish boys who did everything in their power to make my life miserable. They teased me about being Jewish, having a big nose, and being circumcised. They also made a point of telling me repeatedly that the Germans were coming back and they would put all the Jews into ovens. Although I knew that they were enjoying antagonizing me and were making things up, it bothered me, and I started complaining to my mother. I kept asking her to go back to the city since the Germans had not come back; however, she was still paralyzed with fear. To her credit, she said something to the farmer's wife about the boys picking on me—my two tormentors backed off. We finally packed up our stuff and went back to the city. I am not sure which of us was more eager to get rid of the other. The experience with these Polish peasants and other incidents later in life convinced me that anti-Semitism is imbricated in the Polish DNA.

As I look back on my Holocaust experience, I feel that, at times, my hatred of the Poles has been greater than my dislike of the Germans. Years later, when I would be asked if I ever thought of going back to visit Wilno, my answer was always the same—a resounding "no." I do not regret my decision because when I talked to other survivors that went back, they invariably reported how poorly the Poles treated them. They related stories about not being allowed to visit their former homes because the current occupants were afraid that the visitors would come back to reclaim their former residences. I have read that currently there are ten thousand Jews in Poland and that most of them say that they are comfortable and plan to stay. That kind of decision is extremely difficult for me to comprehend. I would leave Poland the first chance I had—and we did.

My enduring memory of our brief stay with this farm family was that every evening after bathing their children, the mother would use a knife to kill the lice in their children's hair. Being there and seeing that ritual every night resulted in my always feeling dirty and my skin crawling.

Coming back to the now familiar Wilno was a relief. We met some other Jewish people and shared war stories. My mother found a nice apartment on a small side street, Garbarska Street. It was close to a park and within walking distance of the Vilia River, which bisected the city. We were on Cathedral Square with a big, beautiful church and the remnants of an old castle. There was another hill with three crosses, which used to scare me when I was little, but now I was able to play there without fear. The presence of crosses next to me elicited a fearful response that the Poles and Germans were coming after me to do harm. There were times that I would go with my friends to a bridge over the Vilia River to look for bodies float by. I guess the fascination with death was ever-present.

The first few months after the war probably represented the first semi normal period of my childhood. During this period, I was able to be a child and do the things that children do. Until now it seemed that I spent most of my time in the company of adults and as a result, I grew up a little faster than I was supposed to and became a miniature adult. The result was unevenness developmentally. Cognitively I was ahead in some areas of my psyche while in other areas I was emotionally immature. This was probably the first period in my life during which I attended school for a consistently uninterrupted stretch of time. I picked up the Russian taught at the school quickly since I have always had a knack for languages. I liked school and did well. I remember an older lady who was my teacher telling my mother that I was a good student.

Drawing was and is one of my favorite activities. I used to draw a lot when I was in school, until a teacher asked me why I drew such unpleasant and depressing pictures. It seemed that most of the drawings were of concentration camps, people being shot, and people being hanged. I did not respond to her excellent observation because I was not about to tell her my life history—I did not think that she would understand, as she was not a survivor.

While this period of my life was generally pleasant, stable, and enjoyable, there was one painful and humiliating experience that I am unable to forget. I was home alone as usual, sick in bed with an upset stomach. I do not remember if the door to our apartment was locked. Suddenly, two Russian soldiers appeared in our apartment and started to remove coats and jackets from the closet in the bedroom. I started to scream for our next-door neighbors, but the soldiers threatened to hurt me. I did not stop screaming but they took off before someone came. When my mother came home, she talked to the police, which meant nothing, as looting by Russian soldiers was commonplace. I think that sometimes they were better at looting than they were at fighting. For weeks I expected that they would come back and finish looting our apartment, but they never did. I had a fantasy that I scared them off, but I doubt that my screaming made a difference.

During this period, we occasionally saw groups of German prisoners of war. They looked tired and disheveled, unshaven, and malnourished. That did not stop us from chasing after them, throwing rocks and yelling "Deutschland kaput," which meant "Germany is dead." The Russian guards did not stop us; they enjoyed the spectacle, but after a while the activity got boring and we stopped. Revenge fantasies are only satisfying briefly; after a while they become boring and devoid of significant feelings.

My experiences interacting with peers were limited because I spent the bulk of my time interacting with adults. Consequently, my social skills with children my own age were poor. There is one painful incident that illustrates the dark side of my character, specifically my inability to control my anger. I still cringe to this day when I recall the incident.

Across the hall in our apartment building lived a woman with her eight-year-old daughter, Marina. They were both survivors and my mother was friendly with them. Marina and I played occasionally and most of the time we got along well. However, one day we got into an argument that included her teasing me, so I grabbed a rock and threw it at her. It hit her above the right eye. She was bleeding and started to cry. I became terrified that I killed her, so I ran away and hid in the basement. My mother found me, made me apologize, and restricted me to the apartment for the next three days. I was too embarrassed to face Marina and never played with her again. This incident is strong evidence of my struggle to contain my seething anger. Throwing rocks was a favorite weapon, especially at people that could not or would not fight back. I became somewhat of a bully.

Many years later I recognized Marina, now a grown woman. I saw her at Michael Reese Hospital in Chicago, where I was a psychiatry resident; her husband was a resident in internal medicine. After all these years this incident stayed with me, so I introduced myself. She had a vague recollection of who I was given that we were both survivors who lived in the same building. Fortunately, she had no recollection of the incident.

During this semi calm and peaceful time there were harbingers of normality. The war ended and there were parades and celebrations. The population of Wilno was an amalgam of Poles and Lithuanians, with a gradual increase in the number of Jews. While life seemed peaceful on the surface, there was the underlying anxiety that at any moment something bad and anti-Jewish could erupt. The Poles were restless because Wilno, which was part of Poland before the war, now became a part of Russia and eventually, a part of Lithuania. There were also atrocities committed against Jews in various parts of Poland even after the war, so while there was no official government policy to harass Jews, we did not feel safe.

7

I HAVE A STEPFATHER

(1946)

ONE SPRING DAY AS I was playing outside with friends, I noticed two men who were former Russian soldiers in partial military uniforms walking down the street who then went into our building. One was tall and walked with a limp while the other was short and squat. Little did I know that from then on there was going to be a significant change in my life.

Dan Garberowicz was in his early thirties; he was the tall one, born in Odessa Russia but had spent most of his adult life in the small village of Kimelishok outside of Wilno. His family was in the fur business and he had three brothers. Two of the brothers died in the Holocaust—however, one was a partisan, a guerrilla fighter, and he survived. Dan survived because he retreated with the Russian troops when they were soundly defeated by the German onslaught. He had a wife and a daughter who were killed by the Nazis. He never talked about them, so we did not know when and how they died. There must have been an unwritten compact in which my mother and he never talked about their previous marriages. If they did ever talk about the past, I assumed it was a part of them getting to know each other and was done privately. Ignoring the past was commonplace because of the pain of loss.

My mother had not had a relationship with a man, whether emotional or physical, for the previous six years, so she was ready to get involved again. Dan went after her because she was attractive and had a more impressive educational background along with financial resources. He was a gregarious extrovert, who was a smooth talker; my mother responded. Dan talked frequently about his three brothers, whom he described as fearless tough guys who were never afraid to fight the "goyim." He also talked at great length about his experiences in the Russian army. He was in charge of a howitzer unit and was involved in numerous battles. He was wounded twice, once at the battle of Orel in Russia and once at the Battle of Konigsberg in Prussia. He showed off his medals from the war—however, I found out that everybody who served in the Russian army was automatically a recipient of numerous medals.

At the same time there was another man who was also interested in my mother; Slocki was thin, bald, and I did not like him even though he was very nice to me. I thought that he was insincere and being nice only because he was courting my mother. The other former soldier who accompanied Dan was there as a friend of Dan's; he was not interested in my mother. There was no question that my mother was attracted to Dan. How much they loved each other is not clear but it was the coming together of two lonely people who experienced major losses as a result of the war. What was striking was that these two intelligent individuals never dealt openly with the major losses they suffered in their lives. This became a common defense among Holocaust survivors as they cast off pre-Holocaust elements of their lives and focused completely on the present. Part of what brought them together was their mutual loneliness. After a brief courtship they were married and suddenly I had a father. At least I think that they were married—I never heard any details about the actual event. My believing that my mother did not have any definitive evidence of her marriage to Dan may have been the result of my ongoing fantasies and wishes that my real father would appear. They may have gotten the appropriate certificates of marriage, but there was no formal wedding or religious ceremony.

My mother and Dan got along well in the beginning, but soon there were issues; the main one was his smoking. He was a heavy smoker and my mother abhorred cigarettes since my grandfather died from lung cancer before the start of the war. Dan kept promising to quit but could not, so he would cheat, and she would catch him. He tried to enlist me as his confidante when it came to his smoking but that was difficult for me, and I refused to do it.

I idealized him as a hero. Even though I looked up to him, it soon became apparent that he was not shy and tended to brag about the same experiences over and over. As I got older it was clear that these stories were meant to amuse, entertain, and impress. When I started to question the repetitiveness and the inconsistency of the stories, he ignored my questions. While there were some basic truths to what he bragged about, I always harbored the suspicion that these heroics were exaggerated.

Dan never carried a grudge, a character quality I admired in him. If he got angry, he exploded and in no time, whatever caused him to erupt was forgotten. In contrast, my mother's anger after a fight smoldered for weeks.

When I was younger, we got along well—I looked up to him, admired him, and was readily impressed because to me, he was a hero. That changed when I became an adolescent. I doubted everything he talked about and questioned inconsistencies that he readily ignored. The only lasting resentment I heard him mention occurred when he was in the hospital recovering from wounds suffered during the war. He reconnected with his surviving brother, Simon. The two brothers figured out that their other two brothers and parents did not survive. Before Dan met my mother, Simon and his wife, Mira, took off for Italy on their way to the United States. Dan resented being abandoned by his only surviving sibling, and the resentment about being abandoned came up again and again.

My biggest issue with him was that I had a difficult time calling him "father." Both my mother and Dan talked to me about it numerous times. Maybe I felt that I was being disloyal to my father's memory or maybe it was the fantasies I held that he would return one day, but it took a long time before I was able to call Dan "Father" and when I did, I was uncomfortable saying it. The initial requests to call him Father turned into a demand, which I resented. There was a concentrated lack of understanding by both my mother and Dan as to why this was so difficult for me. I think that they finally gave up and eventually I was able to use the word when addressing Dan. However, I harbored a low-grade resentment towards both of them; I couldn't understand my mother's inability to comprehend the nature of my conflict, which I was unable to verbalize. This was one of those times when I felt that my mother was neither bright nor understanding.

Soon after they married, I overheard discussions about leaving Poland. These discussions were spurred by Jews being treated badly after the war, as there were pogroms (massacres) in numerous cities, especially in the city of Kielce, where several hundred Jews were killed and wounded.[5] Pogroms in numerous other cities took place between 1944-1946.

There was a personally terrifying incident that affected our newly constructed family during our stay in Wilno. One night the Russian secret police (NKVD) woke us up, telling my stepfather to get dressed and taking him away without any explanation. This was done quickly and silently, leaving my mother and I wondering what was going on. We were up the rest of the night, and in the morning my mother contacted the police for an explanation, but they told us nothing. My stepfather was gone all that day and we had no choice but to sit tight in an ongoing anxious vigil. The second day he came back without any injuries and told us what happened: When my stepfather was first taken into detention the police did not tell him anything. They isolated him without food, water, or communication. On the second day a man came in and praised him for his devotion to the motherland. Then an officer came in and explained the reason for the abduction. There was a Lithuanian man who worked underneath my stepfather in the sanitation department of Wilno. My stepfather had an important supervisory job in the city's sanitation department. He got this position as a reward for his excellent military

---

5   The Kielce Pogrom was also known as the Blood Libel Massacre. That bloodletting was an episode of massive anti-Jewish destruction after the liberation that occurred on July 4, 1946. The estimates were that forty-two people were killed and countless others were wounded. As a result of this episode and others, many Jews fled Poland.

record and his numerous medals. It had been observed as of late this man had been drinking heavily. The secret police wanted to know where this man got the money to purchase so much liquor. The question was whether he came by the money naturally or was he stealing from his place of employment. My stepfather noticed that the man was drinking heavily but he reported that he had no idea of the man's financial situation. My stepfather further told the secret police that we were moving to a different city in Poland, so at this point they let him go. The secret police wanted to enlist my stepfather to spy on this person as a reward for his exceptional service for the motherland. This incident—all too common an experience for people living in Wilno after the Holocaust—was so frightening that it was another factor that motivated us to want to leave Poland.

There was a secret transport similar to an underground railroad whose purpose was to help Jews get out of Poland. This transport was created and monitored by the Haganah, the Israeli Defense Force.[6] After the pogroms, many Jews who survived the Holocaust were eager to leave Poland. While Polish politicians made all sorts of public pronouncements denouncing the pogroms and the senseless killing of Jews, the Polish clergy, which had a profound control of the Polish population and the Polish psyche, chose to remain silent. Before the war, Poland had a population of three million Jews; it currently has less than ten thousand. Poland has the least number of Jews of any country in Europe of similar size.

---

6   Haganah was the paramilitary unified Israeli defense forces created in 1920 and disbanded and absorbed by the regular Israeli Army in 1948. Its original purpose was to defend Jewish settlements against the Arabs. Eventually it turned against the British occupiers and became instrumental in smuggling illegal immigrants from Europe into Palestine.

Leaving Poland was not easy for my mother. First, she had to get rid of all the material possessions she had accumulated and that survived the Holocaust. In addition, there was an emotional and a spiritual attachment that she developed for the place she had lived all her life. These powerful feelings needed to be addressed so that the Poland that was to stay with her was the one from before the war. The current Poland needed to be discarded because it was nothing but a cemetery.

It was important for us to pay respects to the mausoleum of the Gaon of Wilno who was considered the greatest Jewish scholar of the 18th century because of his contributions to the study of the Torah.[7] Most importantly we came to pay our respects to my grandfather's grave. He was the only family member who had a proper Jewish burial. It was important for us to do this because he represented all of the other dead whose remains were scattered across Poland and whom we were unable to properly mourn. This was one of the major tragedies of the Holocaust. There were so many losses that happened close together that when you started to address the feelings about one loss, there would soon be multiple losses that also needed to be mourned. All too often, an attempt to mourn had to be curtailed because the appropriate affects were so overwhelming they had to be set aside temporarily and sometimes even permanently.

I left Wilno with little sadness and a few regrets, but no doubt that my mother felt differently. Despite her intense attachment to the city and her previous life there, she never went back to visit after the war.

---

7   Rabbi Eliyahu of Wilno (1720-1797) is considered one of the most famous Talmudic Scholars. Also known as "The Wilner Gaon" ("gaon" is Hebrew for "genius"), he preached that students should turn inward to study the Torah without distractions. Rabbi Eliyhu was a brilliant Talmudic scholar who authored numerous commentaries on the Torah.

Several days before we left, the three of us made a goodbye visit to the Jewish cemetery of Wilno. The cemetery was huge and somewhat hilly with tombstones as far as the eye could see. There were areas with missing tombstones that were probably used to build roads and other facilities, as the locals had no respect for the Jewish dead—not surprising since they had no respect for the Jewish living.

8

THE LIFE OF A REFUGEE

(1947-1948)

THE PATH AWAY FROM POLAND was lengthy and torturous. Poland was in the throes of a struggle about whether to become a Russian satellite or maintain its autonomy. We had to discard any objects that would indicate a connection to Russia. We were just Polish citizens traveling in Poland on our way from Wilno to Lodz. Why Lodz was picked as the assembly place for our way out of the country was not explained. I had to toss my stamp collection that contained many Russian stamps as well as my stepfather's medals, which I was proud of. My mother's Russian gold coins were sewn into the collar of my sweater. We were not alone on our journey. We left Wilno by train loaded with many hopeful refugees desperately looking for a way out of Poland. Even then, we had the sense that we might never return.

I harbored those feelings of loss but once again could tell that my mother felt differently. When I was young it was hard for me to fathom her intense loyalty to Poland that she always talked about. When I got older, I could appreciate her attachment to the country and the people since growing up and living there must have been the happiest period of her life. However, what I found so revealing was that, despite her intense attachment, she never chose to go back. She talked about going back, but never in a serious or committed way. I was surprised that she traveled to many countries but never her beloved Poland.

The train ride from Wilno to Lodz was slow with frequent stops to be boarded and searched by Russian soldiers. I had no idea what they were looking for but whatever it was they never found it. Lodz was a dreary, depressed-looking city with numerous bombed out buildings. We were assigned a dingy apartment with the reassurance that our stay would be brief. We stayed in Lodz a month and I have few memories. I remember my parents meeting with other refugees and having frequent discussions and speculations as to where we go next and how we would get there. The pervasive boredom led to excessive speculation.

The members of the Haganah who were in charge of this operation were hardly ever seen and when they materialized, they were no different than the rest of us. Once again, we got on a train in the middle of the night. This train ride was fast, smooth, and nonstop. The next day we arrived in some town where we were divided into small groups and walked for a long time. It was hot and sunny; the only lasting memory was that there was a soldier on a bicycle leading each group. The soldier's uniform was neither Polish nor Russian; somebody said that the soldiers were Czechoslovakian.

After walking for what seemed like forever, we got on a train once again and entered the city of Prague. Little did I appreciate at the time that someday as an adult, Prague would become one of my favorite cities in the world. One of the big attractions of Prague was that it had so much Jewish history and culture. We stayed in Prague overnight, assembled in a large warehouse, and then boarded a train once again, this time to Vienna. We stayed in Vienna a couple days. Bombs had destroyed all the buildings in the city, so where we were was the only place where a building was standing. I recall sleeping on the hard floor and getting one blanket that made it a cold and uncomfortable night.

Even though I got to travel through two of the most attractive cities in Europe, I never had the chance to explore or enjoy them. Since Vienna had been totally demolished, I did not miss much.

I remember the border crossings, from Czechoslovakia to Austria. Even that one did not register as a complete picture but rather a series of black and white snapshots. It was nighttime, pitch-black, and this time I was stumbling between my parents, probably a function of too much clothing. We were climbing up a steep hill amid a grove of trees. Then we were next to a barbed wire fence. The fence suddenly opened up and we had to rush through it to the other side. A big burly man in a leather coat hurried us to the highway, where trucks were waiting. We rode for several hours and I slept most of the time.

In our frantic movements across Europe we sneaked across two borders, from Czechoslovakia to Austria and from Austria to Germany. While Vienna looked like a mass of rubble, the Austrian countryside was beautiful. Our destination was the city of Stayer located next to the Tyrolean Alps. We stayed in Stayer about a month and the only things that stood out were snow-capped mountains in the background and the comfortable accommodations. I had a difficult time warming up to

Austrians because in my mind they were just like the Germans, guilty of the same atrocities.

From Stayer we were sent to a place called Cham. It was a huge camp, which became a distribution place for refugees to be transferred to Displaced Persons camps in the American Zone in Germany. Cham was the essence of a refugee camp with thousands of tan tents spread out over a huge flat field. The good thing about Cham was that there were lots of people and lots of kids to play with. The other positive was the HIAS (Hebrew Immigration Aid Society), which gave us little boxes of goodies. Frequently these included crayons, pencils, erasers, little notebooks, candy, and bubble gum, a new treat for us, invented by the Americans. The downside of Cham was that it rained the entire time we were there, and since we stayed in tents, the floors became a quagmire of mud.

During our stay in Cham of just a couple of months, our status and identity as refugees was clarified and emphasized. The camp was the prototypical refugee camp with tents as far as the eye could see. It was packed with people and there were many children running around searching for something to do. We had to line up for meals three times a day, and the food ranged from mediocre to awful. There was nothing to do as everyone was in transition waiting for his or her next destination. There was no way to fill the time, as there were no movies, no books, and no organized meetings or activities. I guess we were expected to just exist. Looking back, I am unable to say that I enjoyed my stay there. As a refugee, you are in a helpless position and at the mercy of others.

My stepfather had a cousin who happened to be in Cham at the same time. The place became a distribution pipeline for refugees. I happened to run into the cousin as I was playing outside. I greeted him but he ignored me. I was surprised and later mentioned it to my stepfather. He angrily said not to bother with him because he is a bad person. When I asked what made him bad, I did not get a response. I guess my stepfather was more complicated than I realized. It wasn't until years later that I realized the pain that he was struggling with from the many losses he never talked about.

The anxiety we experienced at Cham was based on not knowing how long we were going to be there. Where would we be going next? When would we be getting out of this place? It was one of those situations where no one knew anything. There was no designated individual who could answer our questions. The people who ran this operation were hardly ever seen and when we noticed them, they disappeared like ghosts. Finally, the word came that we were going to a town and another camp called Wetzlar, close to Frankfurt in a province called Hessen in northern Germany.

9

WETZLAR

(1947-1949)

WETZLAR WAS A TYPICAL GERMAN town of forty thousand people. It was clean, orderly, and suffered minimal damage during the war. The people were generally friendly and self-sufficient, riding their bicycles to and from work. For many people, the main industry was the Leica Camera factory; their bicycle parking lot was full during the day and empty at night. The factory was not bombed even though it had contributed to the war effort. I assume they made telescoping lenses for rifles and probably airplanes. Before we left Wetzlar we bought a Leica camera that my parents used for many years. We kept it as a memento from my parents' life in in the Displaced Persons camp—I still have it.

The camp was several kilometers from Wetzlar, surrounded by heavily wooded hills, interspersed with waterfalls. The area was very attractive, and we spent a lot of time playing in those woods when the weather was pleasant. Occasionally we became frightened when someone would mention the possibility that there were German soldiers hiding in the woods who had refused to surrender, even though it was two years since Germany surrendered to the Allies. Even though such fantasies seemed ridiculous, even then, we chose not to venture too deep into the woods around the camp. We felt that the German soldiers were similar to the Japanese who continued to fight the Allies after the war was over.

The camp was well maintained; the large gray barracks were clean and empty when we arrived. I don't remember whether the rooms were furnished, or if the Americans supplied us with furniture. Food was readily available in large mess halls, but people usually chose to bring food to their rooms. One could also purchase food in the camp and in town using marks.

The camp had previously housed German Air Force personnel who were probably treated well and did not lack for amenities.

There occurred an incident that immediately threw the camp into an uproar. In one of the rooms a large tin can was found full of bars of white soap. The lettering on the bars was "RIF" which may have meant "reine Juden fets" (clean Jewish fat); in other words, the possibility occurred that this soap may have been made from concentration camp victims. If that were the case, what do we do with it? Do we conduct a regular Jewish burial? Do we discard it? Or do we do something else? It was eventually realized that "RIF" stood for something akin to a factory logo and that it was not made from concentration camp victims. Nevertheless, the soap was never used by anyone in camp and eventually disappeared.

When the camp first opened it had a population of eight thousand people. As people slowly dispersed, and by the time we left two years later, there were only fifteen hundred. People were able to emigrate to

Israel, the United States, Canada, Australia, and South America. I am assuming that some people chose to remain in Germany as getting into the United States was extremely difficult.

As the camp became more crowded two single men were assigned to share the room with us. One was a concentration camp survivor who was trying to deal with numerous injuries sustained from his camp experience. He was very subdued, shared very little about his life, and kept to himself. He was friendless and lonely. The other person was a former Russian soldier who was outgoing and gregarious. Soon after arriving in camp he connected with single women and our only complaint was his getting in late at night and waking us.

From the beginning the camp was well organized; within two weeks of getting there I was enrolled in the camp school. Because I was ten years old, I started school in the fourth grade. I was exposed to minimal schooling in the Ghetto and after the war. As a result, I had learned some Yiddish in the Ghetto and limited learning of Russian after the liberation. In the camp school it was all Hebrew as English was not taught. So how and why I was assigned to begin my formal education in the fourth grade was not clear, except that it seemed appropriate because of my age.

The teachers were of two types. The first group was comprised of teachers from Israel, hence the strong Hebrew influences—they made sure we connected with Israel (then Palestine) and urged us to make the Alia, and go live there.[8] The other group of teachers was Holocaust survivors who taught math and science. The two groups were not harmonious and instead very competitive. Despite the subtle politics

---

8   "Alia" means elevation; to go live in Israel as a higher purpose.

I had a good experience, perhaps because it was my first experience of academic continuity. I also realized that I was a good student and enjoyed school and learning. Generally, the teachers were good and they seemed committed to their profession. Once Israel was declared a state in 1948, the Israeli "schlichim" (messengers) assumed the upper hand. Even though they were supposed to teach, their main job was to indoctrinate us about all the good things that Israel had to offer and encourage us to go there.

In her wish to make sure that I was healthy and received the proper nourishment, my mother decided to register me as two years younger than I was. At that time, no one would have cared, and documents would have been forged that authenticated my age as ten instead of twelve. The advantage to that was that I would receive larger portions of milk. While at first glance it seemed like a good thing, it eventually became an administrative problem that has haunted me all of my adult life. It became a problem because on my naturalization papers I was registered as two years younger than I was. I was born on December 15, 1936; however, on the only official document at my disposal I was listed as having been born December 15, 1938.

This was always an issue during registration at school, on passports in the military, and other situations where one's birthday was required. When people would inquire about the discrepancy, I would sheepishly explain my mother's attempts to ensure my health. With the elaborate explanation most people could not comprehend what was the big deal about the extra milk. When I registered for Social Security at the local office in Chicago, I mentioned to the state registration agent my problem and my wish to change my Social Security enrollment to the proper age. While she sympathized with my dilemma, she suggested that I write to Wilno and request a birth certificate or baptismal papers that would certify my proper age. I wrote to the Wilno municipality for such documents, and after several months I got a response that a birth certificate could not be found and since I was Jewish, baptismal papers did not exist. In some ways my mother's efforts were for naught as I hated milk all my life.

In Wetzlar I realized for the first time how much I liked to read, so I went to the library frequently and did most of my reading in Yiddish; as I learned Hebrew, I read in that language. I became acquainted with most of the well-known Jewish writers, which I discovered on my own. I am emphasizing "my own" because my stepfather liked to assume credit for anything and everything that I learned and accomplished academically. He loved to tell people that I enjoyed reading because of him. While that enraged me, I finally decided that the only times that I could read peacefully were when he was asleep, so he never knew what I was interested in. The other thing that I did to frustrate him was to read comic books such as Batman and Superman, which he hated. At the same time, I read Shalom Aleichem, I.L. Peretz, and my favorite, Sholem Ash. I devoured their writings, even staying up late at night sometimes against my parents' wishes reading by flashlight under my blanket.

The seeds of academic conflicts with my stepfather originated in the fifth grade. Even though I have always done well in school my stepfather decided that I was weak in math and needed extra help. The camp school had an excellent and strict math teacher whom we nicknamed "Teva," Hebrew for "Nature." I saw him a few times which was OK, but he talked to my stepfather and apprised him that I did not need any help and that my math ability was intact. Historically, I have always done well in math. My grades in math were excellent in grade school, junior high school, high school, and college. My trigonometry teacher in high school was impressed by my affinity for the subject and told me so. Each time I got a good math grade on my report card I showed it to my stepfather. In part I did it for the praise, but it was also for the purpose of emphasizing how wrong he was and that he had no understanding of academics. Fortunately, he stopped pestering me about math but then found something else to hassle me about that was school-related. I think that his obsessive preoccupation with my academics was partly related to his lack of schooling. It was partly competitive—I never saw him read a book, although he read newspapers and magazines. This was how he demonstrated his general knowledge about what was going on in the world. He never failed to show off his knowledge about anything and everything.

Our conflicts about my academics assumed a schizophrenic quality. While he would berate me for not doing well enough or being lazy, he would brag about how smart and conscientious I was. I eventually figured out that he was a frustrated academic as he had limited formal schooling, making him envious of my possibilities. My mother would defend me by emphasizing my intelligence. His keeping me from becoming lazy was how he rationalized his constant pressure. His constant pressure to do well in school had something to do with my ultimately becoming a doctor. When I lived in Peoria, Illinois, I attended to his numerous ailments as he was a congenital hypochondriac. My stepfather was disappointed by my leaving Peoria and becoming a psychiatrist. When I graduated medical school, I finally gave him his due. We had a graduation dinner in which I toasted him by saying that he taught me that not all knowledge came from books. Eventually he realized that I knew what I was doing and that I made the right choices, so he backed off. Nevertheless, he was baffled by my choice of specialty, as he could not comprehend how one helps people by "just talking."

The few times I raised the question as to why he was so committed to my becoming a doctor, I always got the same answer: that he was doing it for my benefit and that someday, I would thank him.

In the camp school we studied the Bible, in addition to Hebrew. My teacher was impressed by my interest in the Bible so every class period he would ask me to read portions of it that the class would then discuss. I hated doing that because classmates would then tease me about being his favorite.

It was in the camp school that I discovered my interest in sports. The predominant sport in the camps was soccer. Every camp had its own soccer team and they all competed in the same league in the American Zone in Germany. I developed a liking for soccer and since I was not afraid to dive for loose balls kicked in my direction, I became known as a competent goalie and was always the first one picked when sides were chosen for a game. In high school I loved track and basketball as I participated in both. I loved basketball but was a mediocre player; I hated track but was good at it. I became proficient at running the high hurdles and doing the long jump. Neither my stepfather nor my mother ever saw me participate in any sport. My stepfather would always ridicule sports with the question of what could you do with it after finishing school? In other words, from his perspective, sports were a waste of time. The more he made fun of sports, the more I became obsessed. However, he never kept me from playing sports as long as I studied and did well academically.

Looking back on my Wetzlar experience it seems that it was the longest period of childhood normality in my life. The only previous time that I experienced something similar was after we were liberated, and even that was disrupted by various problems such as worrying about being attacked by Poles. This period in Wetzlar was sustained and productive in all areas of my life. I enjoyed school and learning, as well as reading and sports, and I developed two close friendships for the first time in my life. One friend was Sevek Finster, with whom I was competitive because he too was interested in sports. Eventually his family emigrated to Israel; I was envious and jealous as that was my dream. I started to get the feeling that going to Israel would never happen and that our family would never leave the camp.

My other close friend was Schlomo Neiman, who was also an excellent student; eventually he emigrated to Canada. He was very smart and we competed on an intellectual level. I had the fantasy or the sense that he entered some form of medicine, perhaps psychiatry. Each time I visited Canada as an adult I would try to track him down, but I was never successful.

The all-consuming preoccupation in camp beyond sports and academics was the State of Israel. There were Jewish flags draped all over the camp. Hebrew was encouraged. We had the same political parties as in Israel and people were encouraged to make the Alia. To go to Israel was seen as a kind of loyal emotional elevation. People who tried to go to other countries, especially the United States, were subtly and more openly considered traitors.

To move to Israel—to join the army and to fight for Israel—was a duty and an honor that was constantly encouraged. There were rumors of a battle with the Arab Legion at a place in Israel called Latrun, which was a monastery on the road between Jerusalem and Tel-Aviv. Israel lost that battle and there was the rumor that many of the Israeli casualties were recent recruits from other countries who were not battle-tested. We later learned that the story was a fabrication as the Jordanian Arab Legion were excellent soldiers trained by the British; in that battle they were superior.

Learning to speak Hebrew was also seen as a duty and an honor, which elicited academic competition. Adults were expected to attend Hebrew classes. Yiddish was a lesser language; in fact, it was diminished to a position of a non-language despite creating a wonderful body of literature.

Israel-related holidays such as Independence Day were celebrated with parades, posters, and essays about the meaning of our homeland. The Israeli Army was idealized as the best Army in the world based on how easily they demolished the Arabs.

The camp's most prominent identification with Israel was the creation and proliferation of political parties. They ranged from the right-wing Beitar created by Ze'ev Jabotinsky in Israel, to the left-wing Histadrut and Hashomer Hatzair that were socialist-oriented. Just like in Israel, the various parties in the camps hated each other—they competed with and fought against each other. It was in this arena that my stepfather became an important player.

My stepfather joined the Mapai Party led by David Ben-Gurion, who became prime minister and led Mapai, the ruling labor party in Israel. My stepfather was not a laborer and certainly not an ardent Zionist, so I found his choice peculiar. Soon he was on the board of the party; his name and photos appeared with communications from their meetings. The whole time he was a devoted Zionist making plans to emigrate to the United States.

Since I wanted to go to Israel, I felt that what my parents were doing was dishonest, and I called them on it. My mother reassured me that the main reason they were doing this was for my benefit because if we went to Israel, I would have to join the army and maybe get killed. I was not aware that the Israeli army drafted eleven-year old boys. They were doing it for themselves, for an easier and perhaps more financially-secure life. By basing their decision to come to the United States solely on economics meant they were in for a rude awakening.

Most immigrants that came or planned to come to the United States saw it as the land of opportunity. The beliefs were that everyone was rich, and money lined the streets. Life was fantasized as easy; people had servants and lived in big, beautiful houses and drove shiny new cars. American films that were popular in the camps nurtured this image of the United States. Such an image was very seductive and a stimulus for refugees to emigrate there.

As soon as I realized my parental inconsistency on the immigration issue, I kept expounding on it. I had a talent for picking up incongruities and inconsistencies between what people said and what they did. My doing so would drive my stepfather into a rage—he would say that I did not know what I was talking about, while my mother would withdraw into silence, as she had no credible response and found herself in the middle of the battle between my stepfather and me.

The frequent battles between the camp political parties sometimes became physical, so the camp leaders decided to create a camp police force. There were numerous meetings and discussions about how to do it and how much power such an entity should have. These were people whose primary contacts with police over the last few years were neither helpful nor rewarding. Regardless of their origin, the police were viewed with suspicion and even hatred. After numerous and prolonged negotiations my stepfather was picked as the chief of the camp police.

My stepfather spoke well and had a talent for convincing people of his views. He also affected a military bearing, which he probably developed when serving in the Russian army. He took to this job like a duck to water and immediately made good use of his organizational skills. He divided the police force into two groups: one to oversee the camp perimeter and the other to settle internal conflicts. The purpose of guarding the camp perimeter was to maintain separateness between the German population and us. Germans were allowed to enter the camp, but there had to be a specific reason for which they were issued permits. Sometimes they were able to get temporary employment in the camp especially when it was related to the repair of camp vehicles and the repairing of the camp infrastructure. The financial rewards for camp employment were much greater than city employment so work in the camp was desirable. The Germans vied for camp employment.

My stepfather also maintained good relations with the American liaison officer assigned to our camp, Major Daniels. Each time there was an issue involving someone from the camp and a German citizen, the major involved my stepfather. A number of people in the camp were involved in black market activities. They would sell coffee and cigarettes to the Germans or trade with them for valuables. Each time a camp person was picked up by American MPs for engaging in illegal trading my stepfather was called; he would step in to negotiate a person's release and the return of traded goods. My stepfather became very adept at dealing with these kinds of issues and Major Daniels thought highly of him. This made him feel good and gave him power and stature. The camp people were impressed with his negotiating skills. While this was great while it lasted in camp, I think it resulted in my stepfather's disappointment and bitterness when we came to the United States, where he had to learn a new trade and become a common laborer.

While my stepfather was busy being a successful chief of police admired and respected in and out of the camp, my mother chose her own path to success. While she was equally adept at what she did, it went against what my stepfather was doing. She decided to make money by dealing on the black market. Not to embarrass my stepfather she connected with Germans who did not live in Wetzlar but resided in the city of Ulm. She was especially careful in selecting trading partners.

She maintained connections with three German families the entire time; they, in turn, contacted other potential traders. How she managed to put together this extensive network of business partners is beyond my comprehension. Nevertheless, she did well, and made money that required her to stay in Ulm overnight. My stepfather was unhappy about her business activities, but he could not stop her from pursuing her interests. So once again there was a contradiction and a conflict between my stepfather enforcing the law and my mother breaking it. This was a continuous area of conflict in their marriage. My stepfather worried that she would get caught, and that it would embarrass him—eventually that happened. My stepfather was very upset and had to pull numerous strings to get her freed. I did not know the details of his maneuvering; however, I was aware that this was not an ideal situation for either of them. They were away for a couple days and I was relieved to have them back. Properly chastised, my mother ended her business career and became bored. Eventually she returned to it on a smaller scale that was not satisfying or rewarding, but at least she stayed out of jail.

There were certain aspects of my Displaced Persons camp experience that had a positive impact on my life. For two summers I was able to attend a two-week overnight camp in the city of Bad Nauheim, a well-known spa area in Germany. The city was famous for mineral baths and a variety of spa activities. It drew numerous visitors from all over the country. While the camp that I attended had nothing to do with the spas, it was a beautiful town. I am assuming that my stepfather had something to do with my attendance at this camp, as only a few kids from our camp were able to attend. I think that I did well in this environment since this was my first experience being away from my parents. I remember playing soccer and tricking other campers by short sheeting their beds.

One of the more pleasurable aspects of life in Wetzlar was my stepfather's motorcycle. He contacted a German family in town and found out that they had a motorcycle to sell. It belonged to their son, who was an officer in the Africa Corps. During the war he was slated to be sent to Africa, but he was assigned to the Russian front instead. He was killed, and the motorcycle remained in the family's possession. It was a beautiful piece of machinery. It was a BMW, and the motor was encased in lead shield to protect it from the desert sand. The sidecar was detached and had leather saddlebags on each side.

My stepfather fell in love with it, as did I. He would drive it on the autobahn at a speed of one hundred and twenty kilometers an hour. In those days there was little traffic as there were few cars on the road. Traffic restrictions and traffic police were nonexistent. Only once did we encounter a problem, as the motorcycle was unable to negotiate a snowbank and flipped over on top of us. Fortunately, the machine and we remained intact, so the wish to speed did not change. When we were getting ready to come to the United States my stepfather sold the motorcycle, a sad day for both of us. In retrospect we should have tried to keep it and bring it to the States instead of some of the other junk my parents dragged across the ocean.

We had one relative, my mother's younger cousin Noah, who came in and out of our lives after the war. He had somewhat of an impact on our lives. We did not know how he survived but he spoke Russian so he may have spent the war years in the Soviet Union. He was fairly resourceful and managed to get an important job in Wilno. He became the director of a large warehouse that supplied household goods to the stores in the city.

He stayed with us part of the time but was overwhelmed by all the responsibilities that came with his important position. He then began to deal with goods on the black market, which was easy given all the resources at his disposal. He was expected to keep track of all the supplies that filtered through his warehouse. Eventually, people began to question his ability to keep track of things, which included inquiries by the secret police. He disappeared before they came looking for him.

The next contact we had with Noah was in the American Zone in Germany. He tracked us down as he was in a Displaced Persons camp called Landsberg. We were not aware that he developed a reputation as an excellent soccer player, and the Landsberg Ichud team was the best team from all the camps in Germany. He visited us and based on his reputation was invited to try out for our local team. I was giddy with excitement as a relative of mine was a highly regarded athlete. My friends kept asking me about him and his decision about where he would choose to play. He had a good tryout with the local team but to my disappointment he decided to stay with his original team.

The next information about him came from his sister, who informed us that he went to Israel and was in the Israeli army. When we came to the United States in 1949, we heard he was living in New York with his own family. My mother kept in touch with him for a number of years. There was a break in communication until we heard that he was in Florida. Noah was a restless soul who had a difficult time committing to one location.

Despite an occasional bump in the road my parents enjoyed their life in the camp. My stepfather's brother came to visit from Italy on his way to the United States. Simon was a tough guy. He was a Partisan in Belarus in the forests, active in disrupting rail lines and blowing up bridges. He met his wife in the forests, and they had a little girl.

My mother had multiple visitors that were friends she knew from Wilno. My parents traveled to German spas and they hobnobbed with the important people in the camp. The camp director was friends with my stepfather as well as the heads of the other political parties. In numerous photographs from that period, my parents looked happy and content.

I also experienced some good and gratifying moments as well. Whenever there was a political rally or parade in camp, I was chosen to carry the Jewish flag. The choice had something to do with being a survivor, but I think that it may have been connected to my stepfather being chief of police. I did well in school, and I learned Hebrew very quickly. I was good at memorizing and would be picked to recite lengthy Hebrew poems in school assemblies. From all the languages I learned along the way—Yiddish, Polish, Russian, and German—I still remember Hebrew the most. Each time we visited Israel it was important for me to talk with my relatives in Hebrew and for them it was necessary to communicate in English.

For me, the camp experience was a period of learning, growth, and consolidation. Learning in school, especially Hebrew, enjoying Jewish authors, playing soccer, spending time with friends, and just experiencing a certain lasting freedom for the first time in my life was new and exciting. Yet below the surface there was an underlying distress that manifested itself in upsetting and disturbing dreams and incidents.

One of the most disturbing dreams was related to a Yiddish film that I saw called *The Dybbuk*. It is a classical Jewish film (1937) dealing with a young woman who is about to get married and becomes possessed by a dybbuk, or a malicious spirit that is a reincarnation of someone who died and portends terrible things that are about to happen. The key character in the film is a "Shaliach," a messenger who is an older man with a long beard wearing a black coat and carrying a cane. The Shaliach is always present, explaining what is going on and foretelling the bad things about to occur. He walks with a long stride, yet people do not see him. In my dreams, he was coming after me and I was running, trying to get away from him. He had the same angry expression on his face that he did in the film, and as he got closer, I would wake up screaming and unable to go back to sleep afterwards. I would wake up experiencing him next to my bed. I have had difficulty sleeping most of my life.

This specific episode related to a classmate whose mother died. I did not know her, nor did I know anything about her mother. I went with two classmates loitering by a basement window where her mother's body was being prepared for burial. As we were sneaking a peek an older religious gentleman with a beard and wearing black garments started screaming at us for looking into the chamber with our heads uncovered. My stepfather found out about this incident and became very upset with me for showing little respect for the dead. The girl found out about what we did and became hysterical since she was dealing with her recent loss. My stepfather made me go to her and apologize for not respecting her dead mother and not being sensitive to the pain of her loss. Looking back on both incidents I believe I was being chastised by older men for my badness and lack of respect for the dead. It was almost as if the dead came back to punish me for my curiosity and lack of sensitivity.

In the second year of our stay in camp it became evident that there were changes in the air. From a period of settling in and enjoying stability in our daily lives, there began to emerge a restlessness as people started being preoccupied with what was next or more specifically, "where do we go from here? The primary destination was Israel even though things were not stable there and day-to-day living was difficult and demanding. There was the ongoing war with the Arabs, economic conditions were unstable, and newcomers who needed to be absorbed into the fabric of the country. There was the issue of learning a new and unfamiliar language; newcomers that were Holocaust survivors were seen as damaged and defective individuals. There was evidence that the Israelis, who prided themselves on being strong, aggressive, and self-reliant, thought the immigrants were an unproductive burden. These impressions filtered back to us and contributed to the wish to turn to other countries, especially the United States. As these negative images became prominent my parents became desperate to find other places to land where life was easier.

For people unable to go to the United States, Canada became a second choice. Nevertheless, the excitement and the attraction of going to America became a powerful and all-encompassing magnet. For most people there was something glamorous and exciting about the aura that was America. In stark contrast Israel represented a future marked by anxiety and uncertainty. For me Israel remained an unrequited dream, while the riches of America meant nothing. Material things were not seductive while Israel was the dream of the future. The official declaration of the Jewish homeland by Ben-Gurion in 1948 was the culmination of a dream, which fueled another wave of emigration to Israel, so that the negatives became insignificant.

The camp population gradually shrunk as people left for foreign destinations and other Displaced Persons camps. We were assigned to a camp in the town of Heidenheim.[9] This was a small camp with a population in flux. We were there four-to-six weeks and it made no lasting impression on me.

I was surprised that I did not have much of a reaction leaving Wetzlar. Maybe it was because we were going to a similar place and because we were in the midst of transitions in our lives. Against my better judgment we were going to the United States and abandoning Israel, where I felt I belonged for no other reason than I could speak Hebrew fluently and did not know English. My anger and resentment smoldered for a long time. After we were settled in the United States, my stepfather was bitter and unhappy about his life circumstances. I could not help but remind him that he made the wrong choice. It is evident from the various incidents that I had an ambivalent relationship with my stepfather.

Looking back, I could not help but realize that my two years at Wetzlar were a profound learning and growth-promoting experience. I enjoyed school and learned Hebrew as well as Jewish history. I became acquainted with Yiddish literature, mastered sports, and developed lasting friendships. It was hard saying goodbye to my two close friends as we talked about the three of us meeting someday in Israel, more specifically in Jerusalem by the Wailing Wall. Since we were going to three different countries keeping in touch was impossible. The Israel fantasy was so important since it I saw it as reconciliation and a homecoming.

The few weeks that we spent in Heidenheim I spent much time in solitary activities inventing games. That was an activity that I fell back on

---

9   Heidenheim is a town in the province of Baden-Württemberg in southern Germany that has a population of 50,000 people and is close to the city of Ulm.

whenever I was lonely. I think it also had something to do with being an only child; it was my method of entertaining myself. The living quarters were different, made up of houses with four apartments in each house. Having more space did not enhance our lives. We went into town a couple times to watch movies and then returned to camp. The all-encompassing focus was my parents preparing to go to America—the final trip in our journey after the Holocaust.

10

COMING TO AMERICA
(1949)

THE TRIP TO AMERICA WAS not the fun and exciting adventure depicted in films. We had to deal with complications prior to going, followed by being on a ship for ten days crossing the Atlantic—not an enjoyable experience.

The major legal problem was my stepfather's history of being in the Russian army. At this time immigration into the United States was strictly controlled by the McCarran-Walter Act, a bill that brought together previous bills dating to the turn of the century.[10] The Immigration and Nationality Act of 1952 set quotas on the number of immigrants allowed from each country. Immigrants from eastern European countries were

---

10   The Immigration and Nationality Act of 1952 (also known as the McCarran-Walter Act) collected provisions from earlier immigration laws and reorganized the structure of current immigration laws at the time of its passage. It excluded certain immigrants from entering the United States and set immigration quotas based on the percentage of citizens' visas (approximately 2 percent) of the total number of people from each nationality admitted to the United States. It was replaced by the Immigration and Nationality Act of 1965.

limited compared to those from western European lands. While the president had the power to override certain provisions of the bill, and President Truman vetoed it, both houses of Congress overrode his veto. The bill has been modified over the years, but the basic provisions have remained the same. The overriding issue that controlled the number of immigrants into this country was the fear of communism. Consequently, my stepfather's enlistment in the Russian army would have automatically excluded him from entering the United States.

Our time in the camps in Germany isolated us, and we did not realize the extent of the anxiety in the U.S. stimulated by the fear of communism. The McCarthy Era that spawned witch hunts in various industries was just dawning. Specifically, in the entertainment industry many highly regarded and talented writers, producers, and directors were excluded from practicing their craft because of having had communist-leaning sympathies at some time in their lives. Innocent people's lives were ruined by the all-pervasive fear of the "red menace."

My parents must have been apprised of the situation in the United States because they went about creating documents that proved the three of us were together during the war. How they accomplished this I had no idea: what people, resources, or facilities they marshaled to create this fiction was not revealed. It was my mother's overriding fear that I would talk to strangers, divulge the true facts about our family, and that we would not be allowed into the United States, or we would be deported once we arrived.

Once we were settled in the U.S., my stepfather would use this strategy with me when I was in high school: each time he suspected that I was acting out he would try to scare me with the threat of deportation.

Fortunately, I never believed him. Even though my mother knew me and knew that I did not go around talking to strangers, her secretiveness was so pervasive that she was in constant fear of being found out and exposed. What she was trying to hide was not clear. However, in later years the shades in our house were frequently drawn. She must have imagined that Nazi soldiers were lurking in the shadows in Peoria, Illinois.

The one factor that was in my stepfather's favor in coming to this country was having a large family in the United States. There were numerous aunts, uncles, and cousins that extended themselves on our behalf. The one thing that I knew for sure was that an uncle, Boris Lipkin, had a large farm in a small town called Mackinaw in central Illinois; he signed over half of it to my stepfather. Suddenly, Dan Garberowicz was the proud owner of four hundred acres of prime farmland in central Illinois. The farm was known for raising dairy cattle. A man who owned a house on the land took care of the farm while Uncle Boris lived in Peoria. There was a large Lipkin contingent in Peoria as they were a prominent Jewish family in the city. The point of all this documentation and maneuvering was to demonstrate that my stepfather had employment and that our family would not be a burden to the state of Illinois.

Max Lipkin, a prominent attorney in Peoria and relative, compiled all the papers required and produced all the necessary documents so that we were finally able to board a ship in Bremen, Germany to take us to the United States.

In August of 1949, we boarded the USS Willard A. Holbrook, a ship that was originally used to transport American troops between the United States and Europe during World War II. It was a twelve thousand-ton transport vessel that carried eleven hundred refugees from Bremen to

Boston. The accommodations were not ideal; my stepfather and I were scrunched together at the bottom of deck E while my mother was on the top on deck A. Our level was hot and stuffy; it was dark and smelled. I do not know how many people were there, but it appeared there were too many. Since we were on the lowest deck the constant noise of the ship's engines made sleeping difficult.

My stepfather and I spent most of our time on the top deck where we could sit and read or just watch the waves. The ship exited through the English Channel into the Atlantic Ocean, where the ship rocked and rolled. As a result, there were less people in the dining room, a huge space. Food was adequate. My stepfather and I were fine. However, my mother stopped eating because she experienced stomach problems as soon as we hit the Atlantic Ocean. I think all she ate were crackers and soda for the remainder of the voyage.

There were many Jewish passengers aboard the ship and the first question was, where were people going once they reached the United States. It seemed that most people were going to New York. It was puzzling, then, why the ship was docking in Boston. The big disappointment about going to Boston was not seeing the Statue of Liberty. There were people from other nationalities, but we had no contact with them as we kept to ourselves. The only familiar language that we heard was Polish but at this point I did not care who else was coming to America as I felt that the country was big enough to absorb all of us.

The ship's crew kept to themselves as they went about their duties in a business-like manner. They did not know our language and we did not know theirs. A few people that knew some English tried to converse but without much success. The two areas where there was common ground were music and movies.

One of the crewmembers played the accordion so in the evening we would gather on the top deck where he would play, and we would sing along if we were familiar with the songs. Some of the songs were American while some were from other countries such as France, Germany, and Russia. This was fun and enjoyable as we made a connection with strangers via music.

American films, especially cowboy movies, were popular in Europe. The crew would show movies on the upper deck every evening after dinner. There were movies starring Roy Rogers, Gene Autry, and Hopalong Cassidy. The one movie that stands out in my mind was one of those classic westerns, *She Wore a Yellow Ribbon*, starring John Wayne and Joanne Dru. I do not remember the plot of the story, but I remember the song that was the same as the title of the film. Even though we kept seeing the same actors in the cowboy movies we never got tired of watching them. Seeing these brave and exciting cowboys only enhanced the beauty and the glamour of America. People that we talked to were eager to come to this country and had big dreams about potential plans and accomplishments. Looking back, I assumed that quite a few were disappointed about being here. My stepfather was one of them.

Everything was fine as we were peacefully crossing the Atlantic Ocean until the seventh day, when we were hit by a powerful storm. It started in the middle of the night—the ship was rolling up and down on the waves instead of moving forward. We were scared so we went to the upper deck, as did everyone else. The sailors were scurrying around doing what they were supposed to do, which made us feel safer. None of us had been on a ship before in the middle of the ocean in a storm. We were scared but we assumed that the ship and crew had been through this before, and people survived, so we would also. We just did not expect a powerful storm at the end of August.

My mother remained sick during the storm; my stepfather was fine while I got sick when the storm hit us. I remember going with my stepfather to the dining room, but it was empty. I tried to eat some fruit but promptly threw up. I could not understand why the storm did not affect my stepfather. After a night and another day, the storm abated, and we continued our journey into Boston undisturbed and arrived there on a beautiful sunny day.

Looking back, it was all a blur. The ship docked, we had our papers checked as we came off the ship, and picked up our belongings. Next, we were in this big warehouse-like building where some women from the Red Cross came over and offered me doughnuts, which I never had before. We had our documents checked once again and then we were free to go. By comparison to what occurred in the past traveling from country to country, getting into the United States was easy. No police bothering us, no government officials looking at us sternly and suspiciously, no one asking repetitive questions—we just walked out the door into the bright daylight.

Hyman Lipkin, one of my stepfather's relatives from Peoria, and his buddy were there to meet us. They came from Peoria to meet us and take us to our new home. He drove a huge brown car that was clean and shiny; it looked new. They sent our belongings to Peoria, and my parents and I squeezed into the back seat. The trip to Peoria took a day and a half day. Hyman and his friend were nice and friendly, but communication was limited because we did not know any English, and they knew only a little Yiddish. We made an effort to talk, asking them numerous questions about where we were going, what it was like, and how Jews were treated in the U.S. Due to the language barrier and our anxiety, the responses were vague and monosyllabic. My stepfather especially found it difficult leaving them alone. He kept asking the same questions over and over until I told him that he was wasting his time. In those kinds of situations where I was right, his usual retort was, "You don't understand."

Certain things immediately caught my attention during our drive to Peoria. I could not understand why certain foods in American restaurants were named after German cities. There were "frankfurters" named after Frankfurt and meat patties ("hamburgers") named after the city of Homburg. Why didn't the foods just have American names? I was very curious but reluctant to ask because I was concerned they would think that I was stupid or that the answer was obvious.

In Europe I was used to seeing men wear shorts most of the year. Here it was summer, and everyone had on long pants. Everyone seemed to be wearing pants that were blue, like some kind of uniform. I later found out that these pants were called jeans or Levi's, and that they were extremely popular for both children and adults. No one wore knickers like I had on, making me feel like I stood out. I was also taken aback by seeing so many cars on the streets and roads. It seemed like every American had his own car; in Europe, most people rode bicycles. Since every person had their own car, I assumed people in the U.S. must have had a lot of money because cars were expensive.

From what I remember, learning English was difficult. I tried to read the street and highway signs (I still do when I come to a new place), but names were written differently than how they sounded. I was afraid that I would never learn English.

When we arrived in Peoria we went directly to 605 Third Street, our new home. The house was divided into four apartments of similar size although it seemed that ours was the smallest. We had a small kitchen, small bedroom, and a large living room with a pullout bed. We reconnected with Uncle Simon, his wife, Mira, and their little daughter, Toby. They were welcoming and happy to see us. They had been in this country at least a year so they were already natives while we were the greenhorns. They seemed settled and in tune with what was going on around them, while we were overwhelmed by the novelty of it all.

My stepfather got a job at Fredman Brothers Furniture Factory where his brother Simon and another immigrant named Joe Kleiner worked. My stepfather knew no English, had little money, and no marketable skills, so he learned how to make mattresses and do upholstery. This was the only job he could get. He was paid twenty dollars a week. Although he would never admit it, right from the beginning he was unhappy in the United States. I do not know what he expected given his limitations of language and no marketable skills. He did not expect to have to learn new skills as a laborer at his age. He was angry and bitter from the start, but he persevered and became good at his work. He applied himself and stayed with Fredman Brothers for the rest of his life. When he was forced to retire at the age of seventy, he became depressed.

Maybe he expected the Lipkin family to provide him with finances to start a business or just to support him. He and Simon talked about opening an upholstery shop together, going so far as to check out possible locations. However, the idea never got off the ground because Simon had other plans and ended up buying a liquor store in Chicago. My mother was not happy with the idea of the two of them going into business. The Lipkins felt that since they helped get us here, they did not have any other responsibilities or commitments. My stepfather could not really complain since he was the reason for our being here—he had family here and his brother also emigrated to the U.S. It was not long before his unhappiness manifested in his incessant complaining about the government and politicians. He liked President Roosevelt and President Truman because of their role in winning World War II and the creation of Israel, but he soured on all subsequent presidents, even though he always voted Democratic. He liked to argue about politics with his brother and some of the friends my parents made when they got here. The discussions or arguments were late at night and usually in rapid Yiddish.

It felt unusual to be waking up in a strange country and a strange bed; I did not know what to expect from day to day. I did not like the feeling of not knowing. The first few days I did nothing. My stepfather went to his job. My mother sort of hung around getting our stuff in order. My aunt was very helpful; she took me into downtown Peoria to a Sears department store to buy appropriate clothing. Gone were my knickers, exchanged for blue jeans, T-shirts, and flannel sports shirts.

Next up on my agenda was school, located three blocks from our apartment. My aunt and I walked over to Lincoln Grade School. I had no idea who Lincoln was except that he was a famous president who led the country during a civil war. The school was an old unimpressive gray building in which many kids were running around. It seemed noisy and chaotic unlike any school that I attended in the past. It was one buzzing mass of noise and confusion. In Europe, the schools were quiet and orderly. Kids were not allowed to run or to yell in the hallways. On the first day, I met the principal, Mr. Diamond. I could not understand him. He had a brief conversation with my aunt who informed him of my situation. He seemed interested and then he gave her a bunch of papers to fill out; we went home. The next day my aunt took me to school and walked me up to the 6th grade classroom. I am assuming that I was assigned to the 6th grade because that was the highest school level I reached in the camp, and I was twelve years old. My aunt introduced me to the teacher and told me that she would come and get me after school. I reassured her that I knew the way home, and that there was no need for her to pick me up.

I was immediately struck by the different level of discipline in American schools compared to European schools. In the previous schools I attended a student was not allowed to question or argue with a teacher. When another teacher or the principal entered the classroom, everyone had to stand up as a sign of respect until we were told to sit down. Running in the hallways or up and down stairs was strictly forbidden.

As I look back on my life, I am aware of numerous potentially disastrous situations, which I was able to negotiate because the events or the environment was in my favor due to fortunate circumstances. Starting the 6th grade at Lincoln School in Peoria was one of those serendipitous situations. What tipped the scales in my favor was my first teacher, John Murphy, who happened to be one of the nicest and most understanding people that I have ever met. What made our connection viable was the fact that he knew some German and the fact that he did everything in his power to help me. He was kind and patient and went out of his way to make me feel at home.

The kids stared at me after Mr. Murphy explained who I was, why I was here, and where I came from. He also told them that I did not know any English. He asked them to help me and reassured them that even though I did not know any English I would learn it very quickly. He was right. He asked me to stay after school so that he could explain the classroom routine. During recess kids came up to me and showed me how to play basketball, which I did not know. I figured out what to do and when I scored a basket, they patted me on the back. I later played basketball in junior high school, and it has always been my favorite sport. In fact, I developed the need to present myself as an expert on the game even though I knew very little. I soon realized that the city of Peoria was a basketball hotbed because Bradley University in Peoria always had great basketball teams and a loyal following.

The second day in school was a little easier as Mr. Murphy asked me a question in math that I answered correctly. However, my initial claim to fame was basketball during recess and kickball in gym class because of my knowledge of soccer. Within the first two weeks I readily made friends, twin boys Jack and Jerry Beal, and Sonny Johnson, who was black. The school had a racially mixed student body which was unusual for the times. I had the sense that that this was not a religiously mixed school and figured out I was the only Jew.

The kids at school could not have been nicer or more helpful. Nobody teased me, nobody made fun, and everyone tried to help by explaining things when I needed extra help. I had an ear for languages; the second week I took a spelling test for the first time and I got all twenty words right. When Mr. Murphy announced it to the class, I felt proud instead of embarrassed and I knew then that I had made it.

I was adjusting to school, learning English, and making new friends. I was reminded that within four months I would be bar mitzvah. While I was aware of this upcoming milestone, I chose not to think about it. Up to now our religious connections were tenuous at best. In the camp we never attended services and my parents were not religious. They made a half-hearted attempt at keeping kosher but it did not last. We did not attend services when we lived in Germany. My parents had no religious interests or affiliations when in Germany. Yet suddenly my stepfather started attending Sabbath services. I then realized why he was engaged in this religious routine. The owners of the factory where he worked, the Fredman brothers, were very religious. I think that my stepfather tried to impress them with a religiosity that was not genuine. He could not have cared less about being religious and when he was at services, he spent most of the time outside the synagogue socializing and hardly ever stayed inside to pray.

For me to be thrust suddenly into the religious arena was startling. My stepfather met with the rabbi as we joined the Conservative congregation Agudas-Achim. There was also a Reform congregation in Peoria but that was something we were not interested in. I attended their services a couple times, but they left me cold because they were almost completely in English.

The rabbi suggested that we get in touch with Mr. Berkowitz, the local Hebrew School teacher, since he was working with two other boys that were also preparing for their bar mitzvahs. Their bar mitzvahs were much later than mine. I soon realized why: I knew Hebrew and they did not. Since there were no Jewish children at my school, this was my first contact with local Jews. Initially they were not friendly although I later got to know them. I think they had a hard time figuring out who or what I was given my lack of language and confusion about my background.

After three sessions with Mr. Berkowitz my stepfather asked me to recite what I had learned so far. I had started with learning the prayers for the Haftarah. When I demonstrated my knowledge, or the lack of it, my father decided that working with Mr. Berkowitz was a waste of time and that from now on, he would teach me everything I needed to know. However, I still needed the rabbi's assistance to put together an appropriate speech.

In the meantime, school was progressing nicely and I figured out the basics of the English language within a couple months. I also became involved in playing basketball with the locals. I spent most afternoons with kids at the Carver Community Center where almost all the kids were black.

With my increasing fluency in English I discovered that there is a rich and wonderful world of literature in the English language that I was unfamiliar with. We got some exposure in school and touched on some of the classics. The bulk of my exposure to the masters did not come until high school. There was also the introduction to another important class of American literature, comic books. My heroes in that genre became Batman, Superman, Mandrake the Magician, and Rex Morgan M.D. I used to stay up late into the night reading comic books in bed with a flashlight since I thought that my parents would not approve.

Mr. Murphy and I developed a wonderful relationship as I sensed his pride in my progress. He was supportive and encouraging in every way. He met with my parents, praising every aspect of what I did academically and socially. My parents had the same reaction to him that I did, and they developed a friendship with him and his wife that lasted for years after I was no longer his student. He encouraged me to read the classics; the books that had the greatest impact on me at that time were *The Three Musketeers* by Alexander Dumas and the follow-up *Twenty Years After*. I remember crying when Porthos and Athos died.

Before the school year ended Mr. Murphy felt strongly that I had progressed past the sixth grade. The last two months he had me transferred to the seventh grade and if I were able to keep up with the work, I could go on to Roosevelt Junior High School. It was somewhat of an experiment, but it was successful. I had a hard time losing him as a teacher and protested by refusing to participate in class discussions when called upon. He got annoyed with me, but I could not tell him how much I would miss him. I had no words to let him know how important he had become to me.

My bar mitzvah came up very quickly and the portion of the Haftarah that I was supposed to recite was "Miketz." It dealt with the story of King Solomon and the two women who had babies at the same time, and the death of one of the babies. King Solomon had to decide who was the rightful owner of the survivor. He did this by telling the women to cut the baby in half, surmising that the real mother would reveal herself. This resulted in the rightful owner saving the child from certain death.

A bar mitzvah is a complicated ritual, one that is primarily for the parents who present their child to the community as an adult for the first time. For the child it is the expectation to recite the Torah portion smoothly and flawlessly. It is also expected that you give a speech and to thank the appropriate people. My stepfather did a good job in preparing me for reciting the Torah portion; however, as was his nature, there was criticism. It seemed that I was reciting the Torah with a sad voice and he demanded that on the day of my bar mitzvah, I should be happier and more enthusiastic.

For some reason, my stepfather and the rabbi decided that I should give my speech in Hebrew and Yiddish, in addition to English. I did not think it was the rabbi's idea; I think it was mostly my stepfather wanting to show off. I assumed that all bar mitzvahs gave a speech in English and Hebrew. When it was time for me to speak, I realized that I had forgotten my notes and left them in my jacket pocket. I must have done well because the only thing I remember is looking out over the audience and seeing the tears in my mother's eyes.

There were few people at the service since we were in the country just four months and did not know many people. The Lipkin family was there, along with the usual Saturday worshippers and a few stragglers. I'm pretty sure I was relieved once it was over.

In one's lifetime one is the recipient of numerous compliments as well as criticisms. Most of those are usually forgotten. However, one of the few compliments that I will always remember was at my bar mitzvah. Mr. Solomon, one of the elders in the congregation, came over to me after I finished. He kissed me on my forehead and said in Hebrew, "May there be many more like you in Israel." For some reason I have never forgotten what this total stranger said to me.

MY STORY

PART TWO

11

HIGH SCHOOL

(1955-1958)

PICKING UP ENGLISH WAS A mixed bag, in part because at home we spoke Yiddish, but as soon as I left the house, I spoke English. I started middle school in Peoria, where I developed a problem mastering English. I experienced difficulty writing and spelling words one way and pronouncing them a different way. This linguistic approach did not make sense to me as it was different from what I was used to in learning other languages: Hebrew, Polish, Russian, German, and Yiddish. I knew these languages because I picked them up in places where I lived before coming to the U.S. Even though I could converse in all these languages the only language that I studied in school was Hebrew. While I have forgotten most of the Polish, Russian, and German I learned, I am still fluent in Hebrew and Yiddish. Since I did not study any of the other languages and Yiddish was spoken at home, it is not surprising that both have stayed with me. I made a conscious effort to retain Hebrew since I was able to use it when I visited my cousins in Israel. Frequently, we engaged in a strange conversation with a marked dissonance as they wanted to converse in English while I chose Hebrew. To my chagrin my cousins were not impressed with my mastery of Hebrew.

Most of my teachers in both middle and high school realized that I enjoyed school and that I was a good student. As a result, I was able to form a connection with each of my teachers in every grade. As mentioned in the last chapter, it started with Mr. Murphy. In the 8th grade it was my English and history teacher, Ms. Miller, whom I visited occasionally while in high school. At Peoria Central High School, it was my biology teacher, Ms. Kinnhoffer, who encouraged me to go into medicine while I was a sophomore. In my senior year, it was my speech teacher, Ms. Spikard, who appreciated my ability to speak in front of groups. Central High School was the oldest high school in the state, and it retained its stature of academic excellence.

I spent 8th and 9th grades at Roosevelt Junior High School on Peoria's South Side. These two years were socially uneventful, mostly because there were no Jewish students at the school. I did have two short-lived friendships with gentile students, but we had difficulty connecting—we didn't seem to speak the same language. I continued to do well academically and participated in track. I enjoyed sports, but I didn't enjoy track; being on the team was painful because I ran the high hurdles. When I tripped over a hurdle, I then spent a couple hours removing cinders from my right leg.

The one significant event that year was having my tonsils and adenoids removed. I recovered well except for one incident. It was a Catholic hospital and above my bed was a crucifix, which for a couple nights gave me nightmares. I was visited by a priest, during which I was tongue-tied and relieved that he left me alone.

Ninth grade was somewhat better, in part because I spent lunchtime in Ms. Miller's classroom. I was impressed by her knowledge of American history, which she and I discussed. That year I had my first crush on a girl. She lived a couple houses away. I thought that she was beautiful with blue eyes and long blonde pigtails. I admired her from afar; I did not have the courage to talk to her. My shyness was reinforced by her attendance at a parochial school.

The one event in our family that year that really stood out was my stepfather's heart attack—it was a mild one, and probably triggered by our move to a newer and bigger house. For him this meant more pressure and bigger expenses. The one positive result from his heart attack was that my stepfather stopped smoking.

Changing living locations and schools was a daunting experience that made me both anxious and excited. Now there were more social expectations, in the form of groups and cliques. At school that meant hanging out with classmates in the morning before class, during lunchtime, and after school. Not having any friends at the new school initially made me feel isolated and lonely. I would observe the different groups in animated conversation and long to be included. In a fortuitous way I managed to meet a boy from Belgium; he was also a survivor. We connected immediately and became lifelong friends. We stood up at each other's weddings, and I delivered the eulogy at his funeral.

My best friend, Leon, belonged to a club called "The Grands." It was not really a club per se but a group of thirty-two guys that from time to time engaged in sports such as tackle football and fights with other clubs. The all-encompassing activity was drinking beer, primarily on the weekends. Beer was the glue of the group. Besides beer, the other distinguishing feature of the group were the black and white jerseys we wore, each with a diamond-shaped insignia spelling "Grands."

Smoking was another binding element of the group; I was the only one who didn't. Because her father died from lung cancer, my mother drummed into my head the danger of smoking. I concluded that smoking was not such a cool thing.

The group was a curious mixture of individuals: good and poor students, athletes, comedians, and guys that possessed a talent for getting in trouble with the school administration. There were occasional meetings, although I do not remember the content. Some of the guys had girlfriends but most did not. Girls were a frequent topic of conversation, including exaggerated sexualized activities. My particular modus operandi was that each time there was potential trouble, either the police or the school administration, I managed to escape. Some of my classmates were not as lucky; they got caught and suspended. The advantage of being in the group was that it gave me a sense of belonging and enhanced my social life.

My third and fourth years of high school were fulfilling. Unlike my first two years, I thrived, enjoyed my classes, and did well academically. I had positive relationships with my teachers. I participated in a statewide oratory contest, "I Speak for Democracy," and won first place in the state. I had a chance to present my speech on a local television station, and as a result of this contest and my grades was elected to the National Honor Society.

My parents were pleased with how I was doing in school and the positive reports from teachers. My stepfather suspected that I was not as good as I appeared to be, but he never knew the nature of my extracurricular activities. Periodically he would threaten me that if I got in trouble, we would all be deported. Fortunately, I knew that it was an empty threat, so it had no impact on my behavior.

In addition to my academic success, there was another area in which I was able to garner recognition unrelated to school, AZA (Aleph Zadik Aleph), the B'nai B'rith Youth Organization. While this youth group was very popular in downstate Illinois, it received minimal recognition in Chicago. There were chapters in Peoria, Rockford, Tri-Cities, South Suburbs, Elgin, Springfield, Joliet, and Aurora. There were seasonal statewide conferences that included oratory, discussion groups, dances, and sports. I was an active member of this group from my sophomore year of high school until my second year of college.

Manny Desnet, a dynamic guy and the regional director of B'nai B'rith, recruited me. In my first year in the group I was a passive member attending meetings and figuring out the dynamics of the group. All the Jewish adolescents from Peoria belonged to AZA. By the second year, I decided to be more active and was elected secretary. I was elected unopposed and so I became more assertive and vocal. I attended all the regional meetings in various cities and got to connect and develop friendships with members of other chapters. By my senior year I decided to run for president of the Peoria Chapter. I ran against a guy who was a better athlete and more popular, but I won in a close contest.

Winning the election contributed to my self-confidence and I carried out the duties of my office successfully. In addition to my duties, I won a state AZA oratory contest and participated in flag football and basketball regional tournaments. Being so active in the group I got to meet and date girls from other cities. These girls belonged to a parallel organization, BBG (B'nai B'rith Girls). I dated girls from Joliet, Waukegan, and Moline. My relationship with a girl from Moline continued into my third year of college. In my first year of college, I was elected regional secretary. However once in college, members of the organization become more interested in fraternities and sororities and my connections with AZA and BBG faded. Nevertheless, my involvement and active participation with this organization contributed greatly to my emotional growth—I discovered the ability to be verbal and contributory at meetings. I was sad when I ended my affiliation with AZA and I look back fondly over the time that I spent with the organization.

The issue of college loomed during my junior and senior years of high school. It was a forgone conclusion that I would be a premed major on the way to becoming a doctor. The constant pressure by my stepfather contributed to this decision. Our family internist Doctor Thomas Gorsuch, who trained at the Mayo Clinic, was also influential and supportive of this decision.

I had numerous jobs in high school (and college). My first job at age fourteen was passing out handbills door to door for an insurance company. My next job was at an A&P grocery store taking care of an aisle of paper products and then as a checker.

High school graduation was celebrated with large quantities of beer. One last time I managed to escape the consequences of my sinister activities, and attended a dance where three guys in the club were suspended for drinking. I was sad to leave high school, as I felt very cool and competent during my last two years. I have the tendency to become attached to people that I love and respect, and sad when it is time to say goodbye. Since high school was a conglomeration of enjoyable experiences academically and socially the separation was painful. I have often thought about my high school years, as they were amazingly formative. I have gone back to visit former teachers to let them know how I was doing and to express my appreciation for their efforts.

12

COLLEGE

(1955-1958)

AFTER GRADUATING TWENTIETH OUT OF 300 students, I applied to the University of Chicago. At that time there were no ACT's or SAT's. I also applied to Loyola and Bradley Universities. I was accepted at Chicago and Loyola but attended Bradley on a three-quarter tuition scholarship—as a bonus, I could live at home and work.

Going to college seemed like an extension of high school; I lived at home and maintained social contacts with two of my high school friends. However, I soon became aware of significant differences between high school and college. Bradley University, a small Mid-western liberal arts private school, was not considered an academic powerhouse, but it had an excellent chemistry department. I failed my first qualitative analysis exam, when I scored fifty-six out of a hundred. I could not believe that I did so poorly. I was dumbfounded by the results and for the first time in my academic career, I realized that it was essential to study all the time. I became very self-motivated, especially in chemistry: I got A's in quantitative analysis and organic chemistry. I was impressed by the head of the department, Dr. John Shroyer. Dr. Shroyer was a superb teacher who was partly responsible for my doing well in biochemistry in medical school.

Another difference between high school and college was the greater intensity and studiousness of the students, along with the obvious competitiveness. I realized that I was in the midst of a unique group of students that were serious about their studies and motivated to get into medical school. I observed those that were the natural learners and guys that studied night and day (there were no women in my class). They were certainly more mature, and several were married.

In college I worked as a salesperson in a men's clothing store. I was red-green color blind, but didn't know it when I first started at the store. After finding out, I would compensate for my deficit by mumbling the color of the clothing item under consideration, especially men's dress shirts.

One of my most memorable summer jobs in college was sewer construction for which I was paid $2.50 an hour. I loved this job because it gave me a certain macho quality and showed my stepfather that I could handle demanding physical labor even though he doubted it. Despite his misgivings, he bragged to his friends about how much money I was earning.

I discovered I was color blind during an exam for ROTC. ROTC was a requirement for all able-bodied college freshmen upon entering college. This was Air Force ROTC (Reserve Officers Training Corps), which required wearing a blue uniform one day a week, plus a range of classes and marching drills. Upon completing two years of the college program, you were offered an opportunity to become a second lieutenant in the United States Air Force. This next step required a physical examination, which I failed because of my color blindness. I was relieved when I was informed that I could never be a pilot. Eventually by a strange quirk of fate, I discharged my two-year military obligation by serving as a captain and doctor in the United States Air Force (more on this in a later chapter).

For the first time in college, I felt under pressure academically. I had my boring job in the clothing store where it seemed that I spent half my time folding sport and dress shirts. I was invited to join a Jewish fraternity on campus, but I declined. The cost was prohibitive plus some of the activities seemed ridiculous and foolish. Despite my lack of interest, I developed friendships from some of the fraternity members and attended some of their parties—similar to the high school parties I attended, except for hard liquor and more drinking. Dating was a problem as my parents pressured me to date only Jewish girls. That was not practical—there weren't many Jewish girls available, and the ones who were were not appealing to me. So, I fooled my parents regarding who I was spending time with on weekends. My best friend and I dated girls who were not Jewish, and covered for each other.

Even though I didn't find most of the Jewish girls at college appealing, while at AZA regional meetings away from home, I dated Jewish girls and knew that with my history I would never marry someone who was not Jewish. My parents hounded me about this issue throughout college. In medical school they had no idea of my dating habits. When I was away from home, the issue became irrelevant. The only thing they could do is lecture me that Jewish women were superior to gentile women, which was something that I did not believe—most of the gentile nurses I dated were smart and fun.

As I got adjusted to my college routine, life became easier and I proceeded to do well. I took German as my language requirement because I already knew the language from our stay in Germany. I also feasted on literature courses since I loved to read. I graduated from college after three years with a 7.25 GPA out of 8.0 and was elected to the Federation of Scholars. Consequently, getting into medical school was not difficult. I applied to the University of Illinois, with Loyola as a fallback school, got into both, and opted for the University of Illinois Medical School on Chicago's West Side. Little did I appreciate the intensity of the pressure I was about to experience.

13

MEDICAL SCHOOL

(1958-1962)

JUST AS THE TRANSITION FROM high school to college was a wake-up call, so was the transition from college to medical school. However, the latter transition was more traumatic and longer lasting. I was overwhelmed by the amount of work, the competitiveness, and the uncaring attitudes of both students and teachers. It seemed like everyone was going their own way and no one was willing to be helpful. What made it more difficult was that this was my first experience away from home. The only other meaningful time I was away from home was as a counselor at an overnight camp in the Ozarks the summer after graduating from college—in contrast, that experience was fun, not stressful. I discovered that I enjoyed the outdoors, and it was there that I had my first major relationship, with another counselor. I thought I was in love, but she was from St Louis and once I started medical school, we went our separate ways.

The first two years of medical school are known as the basic science years. They were difficult and demanding, and I struggled and did not do well. It seemed that everyone was doing better than me and that my hard work was not paying off. There was an occasional bright spot, including the time I got an A in biochemistry. We lost forty students out of two hundred during the first year; that knowledge was frightening and disheartening to me. However, based on a subjective self-assessment, none of that mattered, but it still made me uneasy. I was struggling in physiology; the two students my partner and I were assigned to work with in physiology lab seemed like geniuses compared to us. As it turned out they were at the top of the class, but at the time we did not know that. I did not enjoy anatomy; combined with my color blindness, practical exams were difficult because you had to identify red marks on bones and soft tissues. Fortunately, the instructor had pity on me: he took me out of the line and helped me navigate the test.

There were environmental issues which contributed to my feeling at a disadvantage. Classmates that had access to old exams via fraternities refused to share them. It was the first time in my life that I was exposed to illicit drugs that were used as study aids in preparation for exams. Dexedrine was the stimulant of choice. It was readily available from a classmate whose father was a pharmacist. He was very generous and offered the drugs for free, which made him popular. People would swear that they hardly cracked a book, yet it was obvious that they were up all night studying. A common—and painful—exercise was to compare answers after taking an exam and arguing over who was right and who was wrong. This was a prominent activity that frequently resulted in intense arguments. The first-year class was divided evenly between Jewish students from Chicago and surrounding suburbs and non-Jewish students from downstate Illinois. Even though I was Jewish, because I was from downstate, I was teased that I was just like the gentiles! We knew that this type of equalizing division had something to do with state politics that one dared not mention. The main thing I realized after the first year was that I was not as smart as I thought I was, a significant blow to my self-esteem. I wasn't used to the intense competition. It became painfully obvious that to become a doctor one had to become somewhat dishonest in relating to the competitiveness of classmates in order to boost self-esteem. That meant that you never gave precise information about how much you knew (or didn't know) and how much you studied (or didn't study). Unless someone got all As, they never discussed specific grades.

Towards the end of my first year I reached a low point in my medical school career when I decided to drop out because the work was too anxiety-provoking and painful. I called my parents and told them how hard I was working but that I was thinking of dropping out because I was so unhappy and miserable. This wish to drop out was underscored by a friend who was failing several courses and decided to leave school. I had no clear plan or any idea of what I would do next. My parents, especially—and much to my surprise—my stepfather, was understanding and said that if that was my decision it was fine with him. After thinking things through, and realizing I didn't have an alternative strategy, I decided to stay. This was the only time in my life I committed to something important, and then seriously contemplated not completing it.

The summer between my first and second year of medical school I got a job as a lab technician at Methodist Memorial Hospital in Peoria. After some initial stumbles I realized how much I enjoyed the work and felt that I could go back to school and do better. The hardest and most interesting course during my second year of medical school was pathology, which covers all diseases. This is the course that students related to on a personal level, because we considered how the diseases we studied might impact us. Even though I enjoyed the course, I did poorly on the first exam. The head of the department called me in to find out what the problem was. He checked my record in college as well as my first year of medical school and felt that I should be doing better. Even though I thought talking to him would shake me up, it did not, and I did do better—my final grade in the course was a B. I also did well in bacteriology and physical diagnosis, which involved seeing patients for the first time. Not only did I do extremely well in physical diagnosis, but I also loved it. This was the first time in medical school where classmates would ask my confirmation of a particular physical finding after examining a patient. After such consultations and experiences, I knew that I had made it and never again considered dropping out. I realized the possibility that I could be a competent clinician. My Peoria classmate who left school in the first year came back a year later; he subsequently passed and became a highly regarded obstetrician.

My clinical rotations during the two clinical years of my studies are some of my happiest memories from medical school. Looking back, I could not believe that there was a period in my life when I considered quitting. My first rotation was at the University of Illinois Hospitals (R and E) for Research and Educational in General Surgery. The attending doctor and resident were somewhat surprised when I was on the floor at 6:30 a.m. waiting for them to do morning rounds on their surgical patients. Part of the positive memories of my clinical years was the result of less pressure on us (everyone had passed); it was a time to take it easy. A student really had to screw up majorly during a rotation not to pass. I never subscribed to that theory and treated the second two years with the same intensity as the first two; the difference was this time there was a palpable self-assurance and an absence of anxiety. My showing up early for morning rounds was impressive. After morning rounds, I watched and then scrubbed on surgical procedures as a second assistant for as many procedures as I could tolerate. Often that meant just holding retractors, a job that was difficult and tiring. Fortunately, I had strong shoulders, hands, and arms from my participation in high school sports. I am sure that there were other students equally conscientious, but I was focused on my routine. This was a competition to remain and complete medical school, but I did not mind—I was prepared.

Sometimes I would show up late in the afternoon to watch Dr. Warren Cole, the head of the surgery department, do complicated procedures for pancreatic cancer. Dr. Cole was a great surgeon, and very innovative.

My days were long as I worked long hours and I loved what I was doing; I started to feel like a real doctor. Although my primary intent was not to impress, my constant presence and participation was noticed and I was soon allowed to do the first incisions and close up the skin after a surgical procedure. The evenings and weekends were for reading about pre and postoperative management. When clinical points were discussed, or questions posed during rounds, I was prepared.

Another aspect of my enjoyment of surgical rotation was the quality of the people that trained there. They were great technicians who were devoted to their craft. They were also genuinely nice people who did not talk down to students and treated us with respect. My favorite doctor in that group was Olga Johansson, who was a lovely woman with a delicate surgical touch. She showed great respect for the organs and tissues that she was handling—if I ever needed surgery, I would want her to operate. Another doctor that I admired was Bill Marshal, who was an excellent teacher and from my hometown, which made him more likable in my eyes.

The obstetrics and gynecology rotations did not appeal to me as most obstetricians were jerks and rude in how they dealt with both patients and students. Personally, my only bad experience during my rotations was with an obstetrician, Mike Leventhal. He was famous because he discovered and classified the Stein-Leventhal Syndrome, a gynecological disorder of polycystic ovaries. He was an arrogant little prick who liked to lord over residents and interns that were taller than he was. Once, when he was doing surgery and his first assistant was called away for an emergency, I was promoted to first assistant. I had no idea what they were doing or what my duties were. Immediately, he was sarcastic and then he yelled at me, followed by hitting my hands with a hemostat, a surgical tool used to control bleeding. I was humiliated, hurt, and angry since I had never been treated like that. As soon as I saw the first assistant returning, I took off my gloves and gown and walked out of the operating room. I never experienced any repercussions.

Other rotations that I had were medicine, dermatology, ENT, neurology, and pediatrics. Most of the rotations were enjoyable as the attending physicians made an effort to teach and treated me with respect, even more so when they recognized that I was eager to learn. The intensity of the work during rotations and internship are such that after all these years the things that I have learned are still with me. Internship rotations are so demanding and intense that you never forget the clinical basics that you have mastered. In fact, it is almost as if they become etched in your brain permanently.

As graduation from medical school approached the primary issue on my mind was my internship and then residency, the final step before going into practice. However, prior to that step you need to pass the national boards. By this time most of us have become confident, knowing that nothing will interfere with becoming a doctor. Instead, we were all willing to help one another, which is an uncommon virtue in medical students. After that decision there is the added choice of a fellowship, which is partly determined by what you choose to specialize in. By this time I was leaning toward psychiatry; both my internship and residency were influenced by that specialty. My mind was not completely made up as I still nurtured my love affair with surgery. I had some psychiatric exposure in medical school, but it was primarily with an attending psychiatrist interviewing a psychiatric patient to demonstrate and acquaint us with the field. I had read some of Freud's writings, especially his case histories, and was impressed by his observations of clinical phenomena.

However, the main stimulus for picking psychiatry emerged from my medical rotation, where I examined patients with medical problems at a clinic at Presbyterian St. Luke's Hospital, which later became the Rush Medical Center. I was examining a woman in her forties who was struggling with chronic asthma; she had trouble breathing and was terrified of choking to death. She had three small children and was worried about who would take care of them if something happened to her. She had the typical asthmatic symptoms and was wheezing during my examination. As we were talking, I noticed that her breathing discomfort diminished and she was almost symptom-free. I chose not to say anything about it to her, but I mentioned it to the internist at the clinic; he was not impressed by my observation. I remained interested, and the psychiatrist that I talked to suggested some readings in psychosomatic medicine. The patient requested seeing me on a weekly basis and each time it was the same sequence of events: difficulty breathing and fear of dying. I would spend about ten or fifteen minutes with her, asking about her children, She would calm down, breath normally, and leave with a smile. After I was rotated out of the clinic, I saw her for the last time, and noticed that her asthma had returned. Nevertheless, I was excited by my ability to stop a medical symptom by talking. I knew at that moment I would focus on psychiatry.

14

INTERNSHIP RESIDENCY AND FELLOWSHIP
(1962-1966)

I APPLIED FOR AN INTERNSHIP at Michael Reese Hospital, located on the South Side of Chicago at 31st street and Ellis. It was a well-known hospital with a reputation for clinical excellence and research. In fact, at that time it was one of the most highly regarded psychiatric-training facilities in the country. The patient population was a mixture of South Side Jews and blacks. The hospital was well staffed with a class of forty interns. I had a room at the intern's quarters across from the main building and was paid $1,800 for the year. My uniforms and meals were free, but I had to buy my equipment.

Just like when I was a student, my first rotation was surgery. I loved my rotation and the people I was with. My favorite person was Dr. Morris Parker, the best general surgeon at the hospital, perhaps the best in the entire city. He was a bachelor who was highly regarded and respected. He was kind, and from my point of view, a gentleman. I idolized him, as did everyone else. He had a busy practice, and I was fortunate to be assigned to his service. The other person in the group was Dr. Richard Shapiro, who was equally skilled. Dr. Shapiro let me do many things when operating. Dr. Parker and I connected immediately when he started calling me "Benny." I started in this rotation just like I did in medical school, the first one to show up for morning rounds. Both Drs. Parker and Shapiro tried to fix me up with women that they knew except I was already dating the woman I planned to marry (more on this later).

The rotations were usually a month long, but I requested to be on this one for three months, making me supremely happy. Later I learned that Dr. Parker requested my presence on his service, which made me feel even better.

My medical rotation was an interesting, albeit an initially painful, experience. I was assigned to the service of Drs. Mack, Mond, and Eisenstein, who were the top internists at Michael Reese. My first set of rounds with the three of them was traumatic, the result of being asked multiple questions about their patients' medical problems that I was unable to answer. I was embarrassed and totally humiliated, especially by Dr. Eisenstein, who went after me with a vengeance. The next two nights I was up till 1 a.m. and learned everything I could about every patient on their service, to avoid being humiliated again. Regardless, working with these three doctors for a month was an exceptional learning experience. They were excellent teachers and when I finished that rotation and said goodbye to Dr. Eisenstein, he actually smiled at me; that was unusual because he was very cold and distant.

When I applied for a psychiatric residency at the Psychiatric and Psychosomatic Institute (PPI) at Michael Reese Hospital in Chicago,

Dr. Parker wrote one of the recommendations. I thought that this was important for acceptance into the residency since Dr. Parker and Dr. Roy Grinker (the director of PPI) were good friends. Since PPI was such a desired residency the acceptance process was intense. There were two individual interviews with attending physicians followed by a group interview. The individual interviews were benign, especially the one with Dr. Jeanne Spurlock, who was the director of child psychiatry. Eventually I had supervision with her, and I found her to be very capable and a kind person. I also had a somewhat special connection with her since she and my father-in-law—a children's analyst—were good friends. The group interview was stressful—there were numerous questions about my Holocaust experience and my relationship with my father-in-law. I felt that I did well and must have because I was accepted. PPI was my first choice, and I was excited to go there.

Every step in climbing the ladder to become a doctor is a mixture of excitement and fear about not being able to live up to the next higher level of demands and expectations. There was anxiety on the way from high school to college, from college to medical school, from medical school to internship, and from internship to residency. While one is cognizant that the Holy Grail is to be addressed as "doctor," deserving it does not feel complete until the highest level is attained. In this case it was a fellowship in child psychiatry after the three years of residency in adult psychiatry. So when I entered the residency at one of the best psychiatric training facilities in the country—PPI—I should have felt complete, but did not. I was in the company of four other residents (Don Broder, Peter Klem, Jerry Simon, and Bob Gibson) and immediately assumed they were smarter and more knowledgeable than me. As a result, I withdrew into my favorite defense of keeping quiet in classes, seminars, and meetings.

To compound the anxiety of being in the company of the advanced residents, I was made to feel small, insignificant, and not intelligent. Part of the training experience must have been a subtle hazing process in which my name was deliberately mispronounced and unflattering comments were sent in my direction. The business meetings of the residents were run quickly and efficiently, and I was left wondering why I was there. Once again I played it safe and didn't contribute anything. At the end of one of the meetings, a resident noticed my anxious state and took pity on me, when he reassured me that keeping quiet was the best approach—speaking up would have been an invitation to humiliation.

I was assigned three patients and three supervisors to help me organize and understand the clinical material. While the supervisors were experienced clinicians who were both wise and helpful, there was one supervisor in particular who got my attention. Dr. Mike Basch was brilliant and an expert on self-psychology, an area that was just becoming popular. For the first few meetings I presented my clinical material compulsively, but he did not pay attention to my extensive (and labor-intensive) notes. In fact, he seemed distracted while rummaging through his briefcase. As I was becoming more and more anxious, he finally said to me, "Garber, you are a lousy therapist." At which point I said, "Thank you, this is the nicest thing you said to me. At least you called me a therapist." He cracked up and after that we got along famously as he referred patients to me when I entered practice.

There was another unpleasant experience during the first year that was a part of hazing. I was asked to present clinical material to the resident group from one of my first cases. During the presentation I realized that I was becoming anxious as people in the room were talking, eating, and otherwise ignoring me. After several minutes of this treatment I felt that I was being tested so I picked up my presentation notes and walked out of the room. I think they were astonished and taken aback by my reaction because I always had their undivided attention after that.

In this residency we were reminded that next to Menninger's in Topeka, Kansas, and McNeal in Boston, we were one of the top psychiatric training facilities in the country. As I evaluated my four classmates, I was doubtful about that distinction.

Initially I assumed that my assessment of my classmates was determined by envy and competitiveness; however, with the passage of time, I was convinced of the accuracy of my initial impression. The curriculum in the residency was a combination of discussion of clinical material and theoretical psychoanalytic thinking. As time passed the curriculum became more eclectic which broadened my knowledge of the field as there were the initial forays in the use of medication for the treatment of emotional problems. Medication has become—and is—an integral part of any therapy.

Toward the end of the first year I started to find my voice and became a more active participant at meetings. I figured out that my main strength was the understanding of clinical material, while theoretical discussions made me sleepy. While others took forever to digest and discuss a clinical evaluation, it would take me minutes to absorb and discuss clinical data. I became aware that becoming a clinician was my primary calling. The first year was laden with anxiety, but toward the end of the year I felt that I belonged. This impression entered my consciousness when I took call for twenty-four hours every month in the hospital. This was a common rotation during the first two years of training. That meant that I attended the eighty-bed hospital and the emergency room and dealt with psychiatric emergencies. One night as I was making my usual rounds on the wards I suddenly realized a pervasive sense of calmness. I was in charge of the hospital and I felt that I could attend to and deal with any potential emergency.

The second and third years of residency were easy as I dealt with six different supervisors that were excellent, except occasionally, someone would throw a gratuitous interpretation in my direction. These interpretive comments usually had something to do with my Holocaust experience. As a result, I learned to let people know very little of my history; if people asked me questions that were close to my emotional core, my responses were usually monosyllabic. I suppose that frustrated my fellow residents, but I saw it as their problem, not mine. I figured out that a certain historical secretiveness was an appropriate self-preservative tool. My clinical work was improving and in my third year I was appointed chief resident of the adolescent service. This was an honor that involved dealing with administrative issues and not just clinical material. Although it was not my favorite activity, especially the hours spent discussing the same work-related clinical problems, I became proficient at it and kept our meetings as brief as possible. Unfortunately, in the psychiatric field people have a tendency to fall in love with the sound of their own voices. In part it may be related to keeping respectfully quiet while working with patients; however, when psychiatrists come to meetings, obsessiveness carries the day. At the end of the third year I was looking forward to starting my fellowship in child psychiatry, but Uncle Sam threw me a curve.

The Vietnam war, and my residency and fellowship, occurred about the same time. In those years everyone was anxious about the draft because it was so pervasive. Doctors were not exempt from being taken from their training or even practices and sent to Vietnam or other places where American troops were deployed. For doctors, the Berry Plan allowed you to finish training and defer your two-year military obligation afterwards. You had to apply to join it and go through a variety of physical and mental tests to get an inactive commission as a captain and then wait to be inducted into the military. You were then sent wherever there was a need. The problem with such assignments was that you had limited control over the branch or location where you were to be stationed. If you had a particular preference the military brass attempted to accommodate but it was not a sure thing.

The trajectory of one's military experience is relatively straightforward. My fate was different as there were no more openings under the Berry Plan. I went to Dr. Grinker, the director of PPI, and asked him to intercede on my behalf since he was a colonel during World War II, and I assumed he must have had connections in Washington. He was not successful getting me in the Berry Plan, but he came up with an alternate solution. He could get me an inactive commission in the Public Health Service, and if I were summoned to serve I would then be assigned to spend the next two years at St. Elizabeth's Hospital in Washington, D.C. on the staff of the hospital. This would fulfill my military obligation and was a viable solution to my dilemma. I was married and had a baby by this time, so my wife and I started to make plans regarding which museums and monuments we would visit during our stay in the capital. I went through a physical, was interviewed, fingerprinted, submitted pertinent records, and was accepted by the Public Health Service.

Feeling good about our situation, I fantasized about how we would spend our free time in the east. Toward the end of my residency I was summoned by the military. I immediately contacted St. Elizabeth to make the appropriate arrangements for my two years. To my surprise and shock the people at the hospital had no idea who I was; they had never heard of me and did not have any of my records. l later found out there was a fire at the hospital and my application and accompanying materials were destroyed. There was not enough time to restart the process—I had to use all my efforts to find the best situation for our family.

With some encouragement and help from my father-in-law I proceeded on a quest to find what that "best situation" would be for the next two years. I decided the best military branch to consider was the Air Force because I was less likely to be sent to Vietnam. What I did not realize was that being in the military with a child meant the odds of being sent to Vietnam were slim. I found out that Wright-Patterson Air Force Base in Ohio was where assignments were made. I figured out that the person in charge of assignments was Captain John Anderson and contacted him. After I told him about my situation, he was sympathetic. I continued to bombard him with telephone calls, and he and I became very friendly. We educated each other about our lives—I sent him a picture of my family in an effort to make the connection even more personal. He was genuinely nice, polite, and patient in response to my constant badgering. Eventually he offered me three possibilities: Chanute Air Force Base in Illinois,

Minot North Dakota, and Otis Air Force Base on Cape Cod. After a quick consultation with my family, there was no contest—we chose Otis. It was on the ocean and sixty miles from Boston. I entered the next phase of my life as Benjamin Garber, MD, Captain in the United States Air Force. I sent a note and a box of candy to Captain Anderson for helping me find the best place to spend our next two years. We checked out the environment on Cape Cod and decided that there were worse places where one could be stationed. We had limited knowledge of the east coast but being an hour's drive from Boston sounded inviting. Our life in the Air Force was about to begin.

15

LIFE IN THE AIR FORCE
(1968-1970)

BEFORE GOING TO OUR ASSIGNED permanent location I needed to go through three weeks of basic training. To enjoy that exciting experience—and to become a real soldier—I was sent to Gunter Air Force Base in Montgomery, Alabama. This was my first introduction to southern hospitality—and it was unforgettable. I was treated to grits, which I hated; could not get used to strangers calling me sweetheart and darling; and on two occasions waitresses tried to steal my money when they shortchanged me, once at a restaurant and once at the officers club. We spent days attending boring lectures, marching, and playing military games. During lectures I caught up on my sleep, and the evenings were spent hanging out at the officer's club and drinking. Because we were paid our regular military salary in cash, the women, usually nurses, became very friendly and asked us to buy them drinks.

I formed a group of fellow officers that included an obstetrician from New Jersey, a dentist from Joliet, Illinois, and a pediatrician from a Chicago suburb. We hung out together, drank together, and talked about the boredom and wastefulness of our shared experience. The last night of training, we donned our fancy dress uniforms, got a rah-rah lecture about the need to sacrifice for our country, and were treated to a swanky dinner. It almost seemed like we were being fattened up before the kill since we had limited knowledge as to what fate awaited us.

After two years of military life I realized that overall, it was a pleasant experience because we had a chance to make it on our own without parental involvement. The only bump in the road occurred two months before discharge in response to the Pueblo Crisis in Korea. An American spy ship was sunk by North Korea off its coast; there were belligerent threats from both sides. The rumor was that no one would be being discharged because of the possibility of war breaking out. Fortunately, the conflict was settled amicably, and I left the Air Force on April 4, 1967 as originally planned.

Otis Air Force Base was located on the western edge of Cape Cod near the picturesque town of Falmouth in a tourist-dependent area. It was beautiful in the spring, summer, and fall but during the winter the cape was desolate. On the base, enlisted men lived in whitewashed barracks while officers enjoyed more comfortable housing. The base had a population of six thousand military personnel. AWACS were housed there as well—huge, old planes loaded with radar equipment to patrol the eastern seaboard on the lookout for Russian vessels and submarines. There was also a squadron of F-16 fighter planes and a missile squadron that no one knew anything about. The only "war experience" that was going on was in the form of the AWACS on their missions along the coast. I did get to wear a flight uniform and hang out with officers of the flight crews. Sadly, one of the AWACS crashed off the coast of Nantucket and all of the crew died.

The base grounds were well maintained and the base radiated a comfortable and relaxed atmosphere. The base hospital and clinic were relatively small as serious medical problems were shipped out to Chelsea Naval Hospital in Boston.

We drove from Chicago to the cape in our Dodge Dart. Driving that distance with a two-year-old was not much fun. The Dart broke down in Toledo, Ohio, the result of a malfunctioning water pump. Once we got to Otis, we were disappointed when we were housed in a small and dilapidated house in the middle of a field. We had to stay there for several days until our furniture arrived. Fortunately, our disappointment was mitigated when my wife was given the opportunity to pick out another house. I had a sense that she enjoyed the experience as this was our first chance to have a house all to ourselves after living four years in a small and cramped apartment. I went to the base headquarters in my new blue uniform to sign in and get my proper papers and dog tags. There I met the base surgeon, who looked at me and informed me that I did not look like a psychiatrist.

I was treated with the proper military courtesy as enlisted men saluted me while I saluted higher-ranking officers. I met the hospital commander, a colonel who seemed like a nice guy. I met most of the other twenty-three doctors; all were bitter about being stuck in the military. I did not share their feelings but instead fit right into doing what was expected; consequently, my adjustment was smoother and easier. Working at the base clinic made the time pass slowly. The main referrals were airmen that were unable to adjust to the military, so the task was either to work with them or expel them.

These were young men that were homesick or upset that they may lose their girlfriends back home. When the word about my presence got around, I started getting referrals of dependents. Since I had a lot of free time—I would start at 9 and be home at 4:30—I started to look for other employment off base. I eventually had two jobs, one at the Barnstable Child Guidance Clinic after my work on the base and another at Taunton State Hospital in Taunton, Massachusetts on Saturdays. I put in requests for approval from the Atlantic Air Force Command since my jobs were in the category of the military helping the community. The response to my requests did not arrive until it was time for us to leave, and I had already been working off-base for 16 months.

There was one frightening incident during my stay in the Air Force. I got a call from a major who was the commanding officer of the missile squadron. He referred a lieutenant from his group who kept complaining that the other officers were mistreating him, calling him names and whispering that he was gay. When I first interviewed him, he seemed like a pleasant and friendly young man. However, as we got deeper into his family history it suddenly dawned on me that he was paranoid. Someone with that kind of diagnosis was not an appropriate individual to hang out inside a missile silo. After my diagnosis, I had him shipped out to Boston at the Chelsea Naval Hospital.

The base was an excellent place to spend a vacation, but in the summer the cape highways were clogged with tourists. About the time that we were on the cape the movie *The Russians Are Coming! The Russians Are Coming!* with Theodore Bikel became popular. It depicted how the local population in a fishing village coped with a bunch of Russian sailors whose submarine was accidently grounded on the cape.

Since we had a nice pond on the base it was an excellent place for sailing. There was also a golf course, but the game never appealed to me. There was the BX (Base Exchange) that included a movie theater and bowling alley, as well as a place to where base residents could purchase everyday goods at discounted prices. We made several friends with whom we maintained contact after I left the military. I became close friends with the base internist who had a serious interest in psychoanalysis. My wife became friendly with his wife—as a result, we ended up taking trips together to Martha's Vineyard.

Some of the doctors were unhappy about being in the military and away from their training or medical practices. As a result, they would express their unhappiness and anger by passive aggressive behavior that often got them in trouble with the base hierarchy. They would not shine their shoes, wore the wrong uniform, or forgot to salute, eventually resulting in some disciplinary action that was minor. Nevertheless, it was self-destructive behavior that at times was embarrassing and made all the doctors look bad.

Toward the end of our stay, the hospital commander approached me with a serious problem that he was struggling with: he was an alcoholic who was unable to control his drinking, and worried that if his disease was exposed it would damage his career. We started to work together, even though I knew little about alcoholism. He was too embarrassed to come to my office for our sessions, so I had to meet him at his office. One Sunday he called in a panic to meet in the emergency room. He had giving up on trying to contain his drinking and wanted me to send him to Wright-Patterson Air Force Base to be hospitalized in their Alcoholics Unit. I told him that I would not do that but that I would work with him more intensely to help him control his drinking. He agreed reluctantly and we got involved in a therapeutic relationship in which he mourned the death of his father who was also an alcoholic but had committed suicide. Our work with the addition of medication helped him get a handle on his drinking, but he was not cured. When we said goodbye as we were both leaving the Air Force, he thanked me for saving his career. In retrospect I have no idea where I got the courage to do what I did.

To leave the easy life at Otis and the friends that we made was somewhat sad; however, we were excited to go home. We learned to deal with crises on our own, like when our daughter banged her head and was bleeding profusely, or the time our neighbor asked us to watch their five children for several days while they had to attend to a family emergency. Both of our parents visited periodically on the cape and they were impressed how well we adapted and our sense of comfort. As we drove back to Chicago, we felt solid and secure in our identities. We bought a nice house in Highland Park, north of the city. I was able to share Air Force and war experiences with family and friends, and my wife was pregnant with our second child.

16

MARRIAGE

(1972)

SO FAR, I HAVE SAID little about my wife and children except in passing, but they deserve much more! If it were not for them my life would be much poorer and more barren. I met my wife, Wylie, in my third year of medical school. Her parents knew the parents of a close friend in medical school as they all belonged to the same stock investing club. My friend's parents decided that their friend's daughter and I would be a good match. Just how they divined that is beyond my comprehension, but their sense was prescient. So, I called her and the rest, as they say, is history. At the time I worked as an extern at Garfield Park Hospital in Chicago. I called her one evening and even though I hated talking on the phone, we spoke for two hours. I had not met her yet, but I was beginning to sense that there was something special brewing. My initial impressions were validated when we met at her house. She offered me a bowl of cherries, which just happens to be my favorite fruit. Other than that, I thought that she was beautiful, and after fifty-seven years of marriage, my views have not changed.

Our relationship evolved into a hot summer romance except I knew that this was more than a casual fling. We saw a lot of each other and went to restaurants, museums, shows, and the theater. When I was on the ENT (ears, nose, and throat) service one of the attending men asked if I had a girlfriend, and when I told him that I did, he treated the two of us to gourmet dinner at the London House, at the time one of Chicago's premier restaurants. However, the most important thing that we did was talk, unusual because I am more of a listener than a talker. I am sure that has something to do with my choice of profession. I connected with her parents and younger brother as well.

Wylie was majoring in social work at Washington University in St. Louis. She also belonged to a sorority and was popular—she had a good experience at school and did well academically. We wrote frequently to one another with plans for me to visit. However, I found out that she had been dating a boy in school and that they had known each other for a long time. I became upset, jealous, and angry because I felt that I had been betrayed, even though we made no formal agreement about exclusivity. I assumed that based on our summer experience we would be a couple, even though we both were dating other people as well at the time.

I wrote her a blistering letter telling her how I felt—that I was hurt and not interested in anyone else. When I came home, I was in a bad mood, but my stepfather was smiling when he handed me a registered letter from her. In it she indicated she felt about me the same way that I felt about her and the relationship with the other boy was not serious. I was relieved and I decided to go to St. Louis for the day to surprise her. My best friend went with me for moral support. Wylie was taken aback to see me, but I could tell that she was happy I was there and that I came after her. After that incident and my visit, our relationship strengthened, and we took multiple trips to see each other. There was no question that our relationship was heading in a permanent direction.

During one of her visits to Chicago, as we were sitting in my car and talking, I told her that I loved her, and she said that she felt the same way about me—it was one of those situations where it was just a question as to who was going to say it first. I did not hesitate, as I knew that I was going to marry this woman. During one of my visits to St. Louis I asked her to marry me and she said yes. It was one of the happiest days of my life. To ask her parents' permission made me very anxious, especially the response of her father. Her parents agreed to our getting married with one provision: that she should finish school and get her degree. That involved waiting a year and a half. She transferred to Roosevelt University in Chicago so she could graduate sooner. We announced our engagement, and her parents had a nice party at their house.

Our parents met and it seemed to go well although that changed later as the wedding approached. My stepfather talked too much and felt compelled to make a long-winded speech in Yiddish. In the meantime, we bought a ring from my friend's father's jewelry store. The ring was small but after we were married a while that changed significantly.

The time from the official announcement until the actual wedding seemed like forever. There were the usual festivities: parties, showers, a bachelor party with a reasonable consumption of liquor. As the wedding was being planned, there was one bump in the road as her parents and my parents disagreed about how many people should be invited to the wedding. Eventually this was resolved and things proceeded smoothly. My in-laws picked a beautiful restaurant, Le Pavilion in Glencoe, as the site for our wedding. We were married on March 3, 1963, and I remember very little about the actual wedding. My wife's cousin sang as she had a beautiful voice and my wife's grandmother fainted, probably from the excitement (she was fine). I remember the many toasts, especially a humorous one by my best friend. The wedding itself was a blur with fleeting images of people and sounds. The music in the background made it real but at the same time the various toasts and congratulatory comments lent it an aura of fantasy.

We flew to Miami for our honeymoon, which made me very anxious as it was the first time I was on a civilian flight. We had reservations at a nice motel, but they were not honored because we arrived a day early. We ended up staying in a motel across the street. My wife and I ended up being the entertainment for the motel guests, as we were a novelty to the mostly old people staying there. We then moved to another motel where we stayed for the duration of our stay in Florida. That worked out well; people complimented us because they could tell we were newlyweds as we held hands the whole time.

I came back to complete my internship and we rented an apartment in an area on the South Side of Chicago called Prairie Shores. These large apartment complexes were across from the hospital. My wife got a job at Cook County Social Service Agency that placed children in foster homes. She had mixed feelings about the work, as it was located in the poor part of the city. We met other couples that lived there and most of the people were in some way connected to the hospital.

As we got adjusted to the environment around us, we also started getting adjusted to each other. Overall, we got along well during the week. Our time together was limited, so on the weekends we would usually invite people over—cooking and mixing drinks were important activities. We would also spend Sundays at Wylie's parents' house and we would visit my parents in Peoria. We tried to keep our visits balanced and not to visit one place more than the other. This was the time that we became conscious of internal and external pressures to have a child. It seemed like everyone around us was pregnant. We talked about it but did not have any idea about whether we wanted a boy or girl, nor did we have names picked out—we just thought that we would figure it out when the time came.

17

PRIVATE PRACTICE

(1972-Present)

WHEN I RETURNED FROM MY stint in the Air Force to finish my training at PPI, I was extremely disappointed with the landscape of my fellowship. Two highly respected teachers and supervisors left for other facilities. One became the head of child psychiatry at the University of Colorado while the other one got an important job in Washington. She was the director of the child psychiatric program where I was training. I loved her and admired her as a person and as a teacher. As a result, I experienced depression. I then went to the director at PPI and told him how unhappy and disappointed I was given the changes in the child program. He was empathic to my distress and offered to help. He told me that I could pick any two supervisors that I wished to have in Chicago and if need be, he would pay for it. So I did and picked an adult and a child analyst for regular supervision. While this did not significantly change my distress, it made me feel better and I appreciated his wish to help.

During my psychiatric residency I noted that almost all the residents were in psychoanalysis at the Chicago Institute of Psychoanalysis. Some were planning or were in psychoanalytic treatment or were already candidates at the Institute for Psychoanalysis. That meant that they were going to be psychoanalysts in addition to being psychiatrists. At first glance it seemed like a lot of work attending weekend classes for five years, analyzing patients four times a week with supervision, and at the end of all that taking an exam. However, the main issue was that one had to undergo a personal psychoanalysis with a training analyst four times a week. It did not just seem like a lot of work, because it *was* a lot of work. So, what was the big deal of being a psychoanalyst? Being a psychiatrist was not good enough? After giving this matter careful consideration I discussed it with my father-in-law, who was a psychoanalyst. I also consulted with the director of my residency at PPI. I then decided to go ahead and apply at the Chicago Institute.

The important question was why I chose to make such a profound decision about the course of my professional life.

There were several factors that influenced my decision to move ahead.

The first factor was my emotional well-being. During my wife's pregnancy with our first child I experienced an emotional roller coaster as I was alternately excited and depressed. Being an only child, I felt threatened by my wife's pregnancy.

Consequently, I felt that I needed help to sort out my feelings about what it means to be a father. Then there was the issue of being a psychoanalyst that meant being at the top of the food chain and that one could not go any higher in the professional status in psychiatry. There was also a certain excitement in studying Freud, whose clinical brilliance could not be matched.

These were the conscious factors for wanting to be a psychoanalyst but there were also unconscious factors that I knew nothing about.

To be accepted at the Institute one had to go through a series of stressful and demanding interviews. There were two individual interviews with two relatively benign analysts that asked the standard questions about why I wanted to be a psychoanalyst.

That part of the admission program was relatively easy and did not prepare me for what was coming. However, the group interviews, which included eight analysts sitting around a table and firing questions at me, was brutal, one of the most painful experiences of my professional life. It started out fine as I was answering all the questions in a self-assured manner when suddenly a woman analyst looked at me intensely and said, "Dr. Garber, you sound too good to be true, what are you really like?" I told her that suddenly I felt like everything inside of me dropped. I became speechless and the previous self-assuredness was gone. I must have passed the test because I was accepted for matriculation.

The next step was to find a training analyst that would work with me. That involved being put on a waiting list until someone at the Institute had an opening in his or her schedule. It seemed like a long wait and I was getting more and more anxious. Finally, I went to the Institute to talk with the dean about getting assigned to someone that would work with me. The dean was the same lady that put me on the spot in the group session. She gave me a long hard look and then with a smile said, "I think you are ready." So the next week I got a call from someone that I was matched up with. We had several exploratory meetings during which it was obvious that we could work together. He seemed like a nice, friendly man and so I signed up for four times a week and four and a half years of psychoanalytic exploration of what was going on inside of me. In other words, an attempt to come to terms with my unconscious.

In the meantime, I was finishing my residency and fellowship in child psychiatry, having done well based on the feedback from supervisors. I wrote my first psychiatric paper, that was published in the *Archives of General Psychiatry*. The paper was a "Preliminary Report of a Follow-up Study of Hospitalized Adolescents." The paper was well received and a couple years later it came out as a book, *Follow-up Study of Hospitalized Adolescents* published in 1972 by Brunner/Mazel in New York. For this project I interviewed one hundred and twenty former adolescent inpatients and I drew a number of conclusions about their hospital experience. Dr. Roy Grinker, the director of PPI, was committed to shepherd the publication of this book. The book was dedicated to Beatrice Werble PhD who was instrumental in the mathematical correlations of the clinical data. The book was extremely well received by several people that reviewed it and so it resulted in a second printing.

The publication of this book stimulated my interest in writing as a coeditor of another book, *Psychoanalysis and Children*, as well as thirty-three clinical papers dealing primarily with the impact of parent loss on a child. I became aware that each time I worked with a child that experienced loss I engaged in a bit of mourning for those that I have lost and those that I will always miss. I have also written three book reviews, and chapters in the books of other authors. I realized that I love to write, and I always found it easy. When I graduated from the Institute the exam at the end was a take-home that consisted of three clinical issues. Out of twenty-three people that took the exam I received the highest grade, with the people that graded the exams indicating that I enjoyed taking it. I passed the Boards in adult psychiatry in 1969 and child psychiatry in 1971.

Before opening my own office to see patients a child psychiatrist at PPI that supervised me offered me the use of his office to see private patients, primarily children. His letting me use his office and referring patients before I finished the fellowship was a wonderful gesture that gave me the reassurance that I have what it takes to go into practice. He and I remained good friends for years to come. In fact, at one point, he had me treat one of his children.

The next step in my professional development after finishing my training was to find an office in the city and send out announcements that I was ready to see patients, children, and adults. My first office was in a professional building at 111 North Wabash Street in Chicago. My office was not fancy, but it was serviceable with the usual complement of a couch, chairs, desk, and a play area for children. The first three months of opening practice consisted of sitting in my office and reading the newspaper or walking down Michigan Avenue and examining the merchandise in the store windows. I wondered why the people that said such nice things about me during my training did not follow up the nice words with referrals. Either these were not honest evaluations of my ability or they just forgot that I existed. However, gradually, things began to change as I started getting referrals that were primarily children from the south shore area of the city. It was a strange feeling receiving the initial checks for my services as I felt that I was being overpaid and not deserving of the money I was getting. However, that feeling dissipated rather quickly.

In addition to enjoying writing I also realized that I enjoyed supervising residents and teaching, which I started doing on a regular basis. To fill my free time, I got a job to supervise social workers at JCB, which was the Jewish Children's Bureau, an excellent social service agency. I also consulted with social workers at the Jeanine Schultz Memorial School, which was primarily a facility for children that were autistic. Seeing a number of children with autism in sequence was extremely difficult because they do not have the ability to give feedback nor to display the usual emotions. As a result, I started to doubt my own existence and I would sometimes find myself looking in the mirror to reaffirm that I was all there and that I existed.

While the above activities were occupying my free time, I was completing my work at the Institute. I was finishing with my five control cases, two children and three adults. As I look back, I sometimes wonder how I was able to juggle all these commitments. When I would go to my supervisory meetings that were usually on Friday and Saturday, I would get confused which notebooks belonged to which patient and supervisor.

When I graduated from the Institute two well-known Chicago philanthropists, George Barr and Irving Harris, contributed a large sum of money to the Institute to set up a treatment facility for bereaved children. To administer that facility, housed at the Institute, a director was picked, and a committee was formed to deal with various aspects of the new clinic. The director was an analyst; three social workers were hired to do ongoing therapy with children whose parents died or gotten divorced. Currently there are numerous facilities for bereaved children in the country that receive much publicity; back in 1972 our Barr-Harris Clinic was one of the few such entities in the United States. There were two other psychoanalytically-oriented facilities in the United States, one in New York and one in Cleveland. Since we were one of a few such entities in the country, when there were questions about the impact of parent loss on a child, we were often consulted about evaluation and treatment. The Barr-Harris committee met regularly to discuss cases and to do presentations on parent loss at various facilities in the Chicago area.

Within a few years the Barr-Harris Clinic of the Institute developed a sterling reputation for clinical excellence. We were quoted frequently in local newspapers and were invited as guest speakers at social service agencies and schools. Our clinic was considered the jewel of the various clinical programs of the Institute. We started putting on conferences for other mental health professionals, writing articles in various psychiatric and psychoanalytic journals, and we authored an excellent book *Childhood Bereavement and its Aftermath.* I was one of the authors as I contributed two articles to this volume. Dr. Sol Altschul, director of Barr-Harris for several years, was the author of various publications about loss. He died after a lengthy illness. After his death I was appointed director of Barr-Harris, a job that I held for seventeen years. I was instrumental in expanding Barr-Harris from one facility to five such clinics all over the city. Of all the professional activities that I engaged in during my years of practice being the director of a clinic for bereaved children was the most rewarding experience of my professional life. My enjoyment of and satisfaction with grief work was partly influenced by my own experience with loss.

My entering psychoanalysis emerged from a sense of desperation as I was struggling to come to terms with the upcoming birth of our first child. When she was born and I stayed home to help my wife with the baby, I was deceiving myself as I started to realize that I could not believe the intensity of my feelings for our little girl. As I thought about it, I could not understand what my problem was in coming to terms with the birth of our first child. Nevertheless, this was the seemingly primary issue that propelled me into analysis. However, soon it was obvious there were other issues that I was oblivious to.

A question that I have been asked is whether my four and a half years of four times a week psychoanalysis was helpful. To answer such a question is difficult because it involves numerous variables as well as issues of self-esteem. If I were to admit that it was not helpful I would have also had to admit that I wasted a lot of time and money on a useless project. If I were to get defensive and say that it was very helpful and then try to answer how, I might find myself in a quandary and deal with it by becoming vague and overly intellectualized, spouting a dose of psychobabble.

Consequently, I find myself searching for specifics that others could understand. So I will begin by stating my primary reason for seeking psychoanalytic treatment. My analysis made me a better parent across all developmental levels of my three children. Being a parent was something I was very anxious about and then realized that I was good at it.

The second reason for the usefulness of my analysis was that it gave me a safe place where I could mourn all the people that I have lost during the Holocaust as well as other losses in my life. It offered a safe haven to be sad and cry, to be angry and vengeful, and to appreciate the miracle of my survival. It helped me to develop tools that allowed me to deal with my parents' pervasive approach to guilt me about all sorts of things valid and created. The emphasis was on my mother having made a mistake by saving an ungrateful child. As I mentioned earlier, after I heard this mantra for the hundredth time, I said to her "that the reason you left your mother behind was because she favored your brother." After that encounter she never mentioned that guilt-provoking comment again.

These were some of the specific benefits from analysis. However, there was one general benefit that I have heard from others, and that was that I was softer as a result, which made me easier to live with. I am sure that these observations were primarily from family members, except for my mother. My parents could not comprehend why I was spending so much time and money to be a psychoanalyst and more importantly why I would be in psychoanalysis. As much as I tried it was too difficult and too complicated to explain. Not only did my parents have a difficult time comprehending my choices but educated professional friends were equally mystified why I chose what I did.

18

CHILDREN

(1965-Present)

REBECCA, OUR FIRST CHILD, WAS born on August 13, 1965. All I remember was that she was big and we named her after my grandmother who was killed in the Holocaust. My grandmother raised me and was an important influence in my life, so naming my first child in her honor was important. I took two weeks off to be home and available if needed. The pregnancy was relatively easy, at least from my perspective. She was a beautiful baby with a head full of blonde, curly hair—to us, she was perfect. When my wife came home with our baby it seemed like there were a hundred people in our tiny apartment. My wife started to feed Rebecca and nothing was happening; she started to cry so I shooed everyone home so things were less noisy and frenetic. We both understood how to be with our baby. I think that the hallmark of our parenting philosophy was that we always agreed. No matter what the issues—food, discipline, or something else—we always seemed to be on the same page. It did not hurt that my wife was an excellent mother. From the beginning it was obvious that she had the right maternal instincts. This ability and talent have always been an integral part of our lives, as well as those of our children.

Early on I realized that as an only child, being a parent was an important part of who (and what) I was since; my devotion to our children never wavered. Even though Rebecca was in many ways a strong and willful child she offered more than enough gratification that being with her was a pleasure. Early we observed that she was smart, outgoing, personable, and happy. The fact that she was beautiful, including blonde curls, did not hurt either.

One of my most traumatic experiences as a parent occurred when she was two years old and we were in the Air Force. My wife was out of the house and I was reading the paper while Rebecca was playing on the couch. Suddenly she fell off the couch and hit her head on the edge of the end table. She started crying so I picked her up to comfort her. Suddenly I felt a warm liquid on my hand—blood. I was never so terrified in my life. I became paralyzed and started screaming, which probably scared her even more. Eventually I collected myself and called the neighbors, who took us to the hospital. By this time, I had gotten my bearings, and Rebecca was pronounced fine after getting stitches and x-rays. This was by far my worst experience as a parent and I was traumatized for days afterward.

Our second child, Louise, was born on July 30, 1968, without any complications. By this time, my wife and I were pros as we felt that we knew what to do and when to do it. Unfortunately, such self-congratulatory feelings are often premature, and you are frequently surprised and shocked by how little you actually do know. Our daughter Louise was more akin to my personality: quiet, thoughtful, and supremely accomplished. She was an excellent student and a superior athlete.

Our youngest daughter, Deborah, was born on July 15, 1971. She was the most easygoing and caring of our children. Her delivery was somewhat complicated as there were three attempts to go into labor and by the fourth attempt it finally happened. The trips from Highland Park to Michael Reese Hospital were nerve-racking as there was ongoing construction on the highway.

After having three children we decided that it was enough. We were satisfied with three especially knowing they were all healthy and thriving. As the children were growing up and spending less time at home and no longer needing constant supervision, my wife was getting restless. She was not interested in going back to her original occupation (social work) but wanted to do something. She skated a lot as a youngster and became very proficient at it, so she applied for a job at the Northbrook Park District. Northbrook had a nationally acclaimed skating program, and with her experience of teaching combined with her skill as a skater, she went on to become an outstanding teacher. After more than forty-two years, she still loves it and enjoys it.

We settled into a typical suburban lifestyle. Every morning, I took the train to my city office, where I saw most of my patients. I also opened another office in Highland Park where I spent about one-third of my time and where I saw more children than adults. My wife worked at the Northbrook Skating Rink and enjoyed her work as a skating teacher. Every year they put on an ice show in which skating students and teachers participated. The show was outstanding with a semi-professional quality. After several years we moved from our first house in Highland Park to our second one in Deerfield, west of Highland Park. While Highland Park had a large Jewish population, Deerfield did not. At first, I had a negative reaction to the town as many of the garages had eagles on them and American flags permeated the yards and homes. I felt like I did not belong and wished I had chosen to live someplace else. However, I got used to it—we wanted a larger house on a tree-lined street with a bigger backyard. We got both in Deerfield.

Our children fit right into an excellent school system. Soon after the move our eldest daughter, Rebecca, went from house to house in the neighborhood, introducing herself and asking if there were children her age she could play with. My two other children were reluctant to engage in that kind of an aggressive approach. The biggest trauma came when Deborah, our youngest daughter, who was two at the time wandered off with some older kids she was playing with. We received a call from the local police who picked her up wandering the streets of the neighborhood. She didn't seem disturbed by the experience as much as we were. In another episode, my wife got a call from Rebecca's fourth grade teacher who told her that Rebecca fell off a jungle gym on the school playground and was complaining of pain in both arms. My wife rushed over to the school and saw Rebecca standing there with her arms spread out like a cross. My wife told her to put down her arms. Rebecca did as she was told and was fine—just scared.

My wife and I made friends with people from the Institute, our neighborhood, and my wife's workplace. Social life at this time consisted of going out to dinner, followed by a movie or theater with friends. I renewed my friendship with my best friend from high school (the Holocaust survivor from Belgium); we spent time together visiting our parents' graves in Peoria.

My practice was booming, and I worked long hours. The initial anxiety about not getting enough referrals dissipated as my patient load was evenly divided between children and adults.

All three of our daughters became active in sports during high school. Rebecca played volleyball and was a state semifinalist in badminton. Louise was a stellar athlete as she was a starter in softball and basketball, as well as a conference starter—she received special mention in state volleyball. In her senior year she was picked as the outstanding female athlete of her graduating class. Deborah played volleyball and was an accomplished figure skater who participated in various state competitive events. Needless to say, we were proud of all their accomplishments and even bragged about them occasionally.

As we get older, we tend to measure our life stages by where our children are in school. Our children were exactly three years apart, so it was easy to determine where we ranked in life as adults. One of the most important experiences as a parent occurred as my wife and I were attending an assembly at the high school for incoming freshmen. I was observing the hustle and bustle of the crowd when I was suddenly hit with a realization. Rebecca was entering high school and I suddenly felt like I barely knew her. I realized that in four years she would be leaving for college—a sudden wave of sadness washed over me. My wife noticed my mood change and wanted to know what happened? When I told her about my sudden distress, she smiled and said it would be another four and a half years before she left. She told me to relax because I would have ample time with her. I agreed that I was being silly, but that day I made an important decision which I observed as long as the kids were in school, and even afterwards. From that day on, I rearranged my work schedule in order to be home every Wednesday afternoon so that I would be available to engage in an activity with my wife or one of our daughters, always of their choosing. I have stuck by that decision all these years, and it was one of the smartest decisions I ever made. Even now with all my children grown and some of my grandchildren semi-grown, Wednesday night is family dinner night for whoever can come; it has become a special occasion. Confirmation for this activity came from my twelve-year-old grandson who told me, "Poppa, when I have had a bad day at school or a fight with one of my friends, family dinner always makes me feel better."

My wife and I have been fortunate to have our three children and our eight grandchildren living close by. Jonah, our oldest grandchild, moved to Seattle a couple years ago but visits Chicago frequently. He is able to sometimes stay for weeks at a time because he can work from home.

Some of our friends have children and grandchildren scattered all over the country and have expressed envy at our good fortune. They are curious how we did that or what psychological strategies we devised to influence them to live here. I respond that if I knew the secret, I would package it and sell it. As far as I can remember I did not threaten them, bribe them, or threaten to disown them if they were planning to move far from us. I did not remember ever making an issue about where they should live. Maybe there was something reassuring about not making an issue out of it, and they were able to make their choices without having to be concerned about our reactions. I assume they knew that we wanted them to live here. Maybe they felt that we would not intrude on their space and respect their privacy no matter where they lived. However, it may well be that all this speculation is useless and meaningless, and that their choices were based on practical issues with which we were unfamiliar. Maybe it was just that the milieu in this area was attractive and provided all of the things they needed and wanted, including an excellent school system, beautiful parks, and the closeness of friends.

When your children begin to consider college there emerges a conglomeration of feelings, which does not prepare you for the coming loss. While my wife was accurate in her amusement regarding my sadness about our oldest daughter going off to college, I still felt that my feelings were totally appropriate, rational, and justified. As a palpable validation of my feelings, after Rebecca left to attend the University of Indiana, three weeks passed before I felt comfortable entering her room. Even then I stood in the center of the room becoming reacquainted with its contents or perhaps expecting Rebecca to jump out of her closet and restore my happiness by reassuring me that she never left.

However, gradually we got used to the notion that she was coming back only to visit—her two sisters managed to fill the void that was a part of her presence. Since this was not yet the age of cell phones, calls were usually limited to weekends. When she would come home from school, we were always thrilled to see her and find out about her life at school, wondering secretly if she missed us as much as we missed her. We filled her in on what she might have missed when away and she lay in bed with her sisters exchanging stories about boys, but by the next night she always requested the car keys.

While the above description of my distress may be somewhat dramatic and perhaps exaggerated, I can offer the evidence of my reactions to

Louise leaving for the University of Michigan three years later and then Deborah leaving for Ohio State three years after that. That hardened my experience and I was able to contain some of the emotional content of future partings, but the toll is similar.

The ultimate abandonment manifested itself when all three children were gone and suddenly our house became as silent as a tomb. The freedom to swear without hesitation or to run around the house in your underwear at all times of the day or night does not compensate for what is missing.

My wife and I gradually readjusted to just the two of us being alone at home and tried to recall what life was like before we had children; it was an empty exercise because try as we might, it was—and will never be—the same.

All three of the girls enjoyed and thrived in their college careers. They all attended Big Ten schools in the Midwest that were within driving distance of Chicago. Maybe those choices had something to do with their decisions to come back and live on the North Shore.

All three enjoyed most of their classes, belonged to sororities, and hardly ever complained about their academic environments; none ever expressed any wishes to transfer schools. The three of them developed friendships with college classmates that continued after graduation.

There was one significant incident involving Rebecca that I found interesting and somewhat amusing. The second semester of her senior year, during which she did not appear to work very hard, she called me with a question: "What do you think of black people?" While the question did catch me by surprise, I realized what was coming. She had been dating a senior in premed. David was black. I asked whether he was treating her well and whether she enjoyed spending time with him. She told me that they got along well and she enjoyed being with him and talking with him, and that he was very intelligent. So, I was curious: what was the problem? She said that some of the boys belonging to a Jewish fraternity had been giving her a hard time about dating someone who was black. I told her that as long as the two of them were happy together, I did not have a problem with their relationship. I told her to just ignore the fraternity boys—who she dated was none of their business. She seemed relieved by my response and told me that they had made plans for us and his parents to meet for dinner after their upcoming graduation. When we came for graduation, she informed us of a change in plans and instead of dinner, we were meeting for cocktails. I said that was fine and to just let us know when and where to meet them. There was then another change of plans: his parents needed to leave right after graduation, so we never got to meet them. When we left after graduation, she remained in school for several days and they continued to correspond when she came home. Gradually, the relationship fizzled and after a while we never heard any more about David.

One of the ongoing questions in working with children is to what degree are parents unconsciously responsible for the choices that children make, both positive and negative. In terms of education and educational choices, parents may have something to say to encourage or discourage their child from moving vocationally in a certain direction. My stepfather had an impact on my choosing to go into medicine. My choice made him proud of me; he frequently bragged about my choice of profession. However, he was disappointed that I chose to go into psychiatry and took it almost as a personal affront. He could never figure out how one could have a curative impact on people by "just talking to them." When he realized that I was happy with my vocational choice, he eventually came to terms with what I was doing, even though why remained a mystery to him for the rest of his life.

When Rebecca was little, she talked about someday wanting to be a lawyer. Where this came from was a mystery as the only attorney in the family was my brother-in-law and she was not close to him. She struggled academically the first two years of high school, but in her junior year she became impressed by her writing teacher. He stimulated her interest in writing and as a result, her grades improved during her final two years. As she got older, she expressed aspirations of becoming a judge. She did not become a judge, but she did attend Loyola Law School in Chicago and became an attorney. In fact, she met her husband, also an attorney, while preparing for the bar exam. We were pleased with her choice, supported her studies, and encouraged her along the way. Given her youthful interests her choice made sense, as her childhood interests became a reality.

Louise was never explicit about her vocational interests. When she was in college, she took an economics course that she enjoyed but that was the closest she came to tipping her hand. Because she was gifted academically, I once mentioned to her that if she ever considered attending medical school we would support it. She said that she had no interest in medicine and that was the end of the discussion. After she graduated college as an economics major, she spent a year traveling in Europe with friends. When she returned from her trip, she announced an interest in attending business school. She attended the University of Chicago Business School, enjoyed it, did extremely well, and even received an award in marketing.

She also met her future husband in business school, so it turned out to be a well-rounded gratifying experience.

Deborah attended Ohio State University, where she had a good experience. I do not remember her being that definitive about her vocational interests and what exactly she aspired to after graduation. She took some education courses and surprised us by becoming much more of a student in college than in high school. She got her degree in education and after working for a while expressed an interest in attending graduate school in education.

She was accepted at the DePaul Graduate Education Program in Chicago, where she received her PhD. She did extremely well, working full-time as a teacher while married and raising two children. Her graduate thesis focused on how children can be better prepared to deal with bullying. As of 2020, she has been teaching at the Glencoe (Illinois) school system for twenty years and by all accounts has been regarded as an outstanding teacher.

When your children start thinking about getting married and having their own families, it is another step towards a more permanent separation from your nuclear family. While in some ways it results in a more equalizing relationship, it also denotes a separateness that continues for the rest of your life. A common equalizing experience manifests itself when a parent asks their child for advice in a certain area in which the child is more of an expert than the parent.

A child may ask their parents' advice about an upcoming wedding while their parent may need to consider their child's wishes regarding the ceremony or entertainment at the reception. A particular incident stands out in my mind when Rebecca began to make wedding plans.

When the bills for the wedding's expenses began to arrive, I started to complain rather loudly that at this rate the expenses would drive me into the poorhouse. As I was going through this litany of complaints my daughter, who was sitting across from me, started to cry. Finally, she said to me, "Dad, if this is an expense beyond your means we should not do this or do it differently." After realizing my guilt-provoking rant, I decided not to complain about expenses anymore since I had two more weddings on the horizon. She had a beautiful wedding that exceeded all our expectations.

Louise's wedding was equally beautiful and exciting since we now had a standard for comparison. She had some very definite ideas as to how she wanted things to be done and in what order. When someone suggested she use her sister's wedding dress, which has been preserved as she requested, it became obvious that she wanted to make her own selection. The main thing that stands out in my mind from her wedding is my future son-in-law's anxiety when he asked my permission to marry her, as well as his nervousness during the ceremony. He kept making comments as an aside during the rabbi's blessings. I found his comments humorous.

By the time Deborah was getting married we felt like old pros and experts on the intricacies of what was about to transpire. My wife and the three girls were going to a dress shop to select her gown and then be fitted for it. I was not able to attend as I was working that Saturday morning. When they returned from the fitting, I could tell that my usually cheerful and happy daughter was upset, in part because she retreated to her room in tears. I was not aware that her reaction had anything to do with me. Eventually she came out of her room sobbing and told me that she was disappointed and angry that I did not attend the fitting. At first I became defensive and told her that patients depended on my presence. She informed me that my patients could be rescheduled while this would be my last chance to see my youngest daughter in her new wedding dress. I made sure to be there for the final fitting.

Before her wedding we visited Deborah at school during her last parents' weekend. We were shopping in Columbus when I noticed a beautiful glass piece in one of the town's many art galleries. She observed my interest with great awareness. Then she called me aside and in an earnest voice expressed a concern about whether I would be able to finance a third wedding.

Her wedding was equally beautiful and exciting, and we celebrated with joy and pleasure. The next morning when we were attending the final brunch I was overcome with sadness, as there would be no more weddings. This was the last one; I was sad that it was over and wished we could do it again, hang the expense.

1 9

GRANDCHILDREN

(1965-Present)

GRANDPARENTHOOD IS PARENTHOOD ONCE RE-MOVED—you get to enjoy your grandchild and spend time with them, but you have the option to leave if and when a problem should arise. The presence of a grandchild is a new lease on life that can be invigorating, yet there is something about that title that puts the aging process right in front of you. Being a grandparent can be life-affirming, gratifying, and a palpable generational extension. Just the naming of a grandchild can become conflict-laden because of competing families, but it can also become an affirmation of generational continuity. As I mentioned earlier, Rebecca's son was named Jonah after the father that I never knew. When she first told me her choice I was overcome with emotion because in this way my father seemed to have almost risen from the dead, never to be forgotten.

My wife and I have been fortunate to have eight healthy and happy grandchildren, ranging in age from twelve to twenty-five. As they have matured, I have realized that over the years I have developed, almost imperceptibly, something unique and special with each of my grandchildren. With Jonah, it was our love and appreciation of basketball, our favorite sport. When he was in middle school, we would play basketball every Sunday and then go out for breakfast and talk. We talked about anything and everything: sports, school, music, feelings. After graduating from University of Illinois School of Computer Engineering, he eventually moved to Seattle to work for Amazon, so we do not see him as much as we would like, but we keep in touch and talk periodically.

My second grandson, Jacob, is twenty-three years old as I write this; he is Rebecca's middle child. Jacob graduated cum laude from Northwestern University Theater School and has a talent for acting and singing. He hopes to make it in show business. He has a beautiful voice and we have seen him in numerous plays. Jacob has a great sense of humor, is well-informed, and is a talented chef. He and I have developed a special routine when we say goodbye to one another. We slap each other on the back, and we bellow rather loudly, which startles passersby.

Next come twin granddaughters, Emily and Hannah, Louise's oldest children. Nineteen-year-old fraternal twins, they are totally different in appearance, personality, and talents. Emily is studying to be a doctor at Vanderbilt University and has gained experience working in a research lab. She also loves to bake and is very good at it. She is quiet and tends to hang back, but despite that quality you are always aware of her presence.

Hannah is completely different from her twin sister—she is very energetic, talks a mile a minute, and is full of thoughts and ideas. Focused on women's rights and how women are treated, she is attending Washington University and has an interest in being an attorney. Hannah also has a great sense of fashion and comments frequently about what people are wearing or should be wearing. She is very interested how things match and how they are fitted together. Fashion design may be another calling.

Our third grandson, Rebecca's youngest son, Joshua, is the youngest of three siblings. He is in his second year of college and most likely will major in business. He is very interested in sports, especially basketball. Basketball is our connection: we discuss teams and have friendly arguments about which players are better. He is a sweet kid who is very friendly and good-natured.

Our next grandson and Louise's youngest child, Jeremy, is a freshman at the same school as his sister Emily—Vanderbilt University. He is also a very bright kid and is studying medical engineering. He and I have a close relationship as we are both interested in sports, especially football. He is very intense, emotional, and affectionate. He and I just seem to relate on multiple levels and we always have something to talk about.

Our next grandson, Simon, is a sophomore in high school. He is fifteen years old and Deborah's oldest child. Simon is quiet, but over the past couple of years he has become more open and outgoing. He is a good student and an excellent baseball player. When we talk, it is often about sports, especially basketball and baseball.

Our youngest grandchild, Talia, is twelve years old and she is a firecracker. Deborah's youngest child, she is very social and outgoing, has many friends, and everyone likes her. Talia is involved in ice skating, which she especially enjoys when it's her grandmother teaching her—the two are very close. My connection with her revolves around game playing, something at which she is very good.

20

WHERE TO NOW?

(2020)

AS I EXAMINE MY LIFE I am pleased with where I am and where I have been. It has been a long and at times difficult road, but I would like to think that I have made it. I have had many losses in my life, which have lent a sad cast to my personality. As I write this, I am eighty-three years old and in reasonably good health, despite having had serious back problems for which I had surgery six years ago. Consequently, I am limited physically and unable to participate in sports, especially tennis and basketball, my favorite activities. However, I work out religiously several times a week and my weight has stayed the same for the past twenty-five years. I used to be a runner, but not anymore.

I still have a full-time practice in adult and child psychiatry and psychoanalysis. I am not as busy as I used to be, and my practice has shifted from being equally divided between children and adults to primarily adults. I am not sure why the change; perhaps people think that I am too old to see children. I enjoy my practice and get excited each time I start with a new patient. I teach and I supervise psychoanalytic candidates (students of psychoanalysis who are going to become psychoanalysts). I have been teaching a seminar on my favorite subject, the impact of parent loss on a child. I get inspired when I have to do a presentation especially dealing with loss given that the topic has been a lifetime preoccupation. I love to read, primarily nonfiction and history.

I would like to think that I have been able to strike a balance between my personal and professional lives although my wife would beg to differ. We have been married fifty-seven years and I still find my wife attractive and exciting. Personality-wise we are quite different: she is outgoing, friendly, warm, and socially adept. I am more withdrawn, somewhat aloof until people get to know me, moody at times, and I enjoy solitary activities. We have always been attracted physically to each other, and mesh our parenting styles, resulting in our children turning out stable and well-adjusted. When we have had fights over the years my wife has been more forgiving than I, but I have never stayed angry at my children. I have been subservient to a strong sense of guilt over just about everything and anything that plays havoc with my personality. Sometimes I feel guilty about being alive. My wife and I have developed similar interests; we both like to travel and have visited many countries. Of all the places we have been, Israel and China have impressed me the most.

One of the areas of conflict has been our "Jewishness"—how observant we are when it comes to basic practices, holidays, supporting other Jewish communities, and contributing to Jewish charities—as I am more so than my wife. This difference is due to how we were each raised, as well as my Holocaust experiences. However, I think my wife has come around to my point of view although I am sure she would disagree. All our three daughters have married Jewish men and have stable marriages. Materially, we have enjoyed a comfortable life as we have both worked for many years and supported each other's vocational choices. We have enjoyed social events although my wife more so than I. Like most people we enjoy films and the theater. One activity that we have both enjoyed is dancing, even though we have never had any formal lessons and we do not move as well as we used to.

My wife and I have maintained the same friendships over many years. Unfortunately, some of our friends have died and some have gotten divorced. With the latter, for some reason we have usually maintained a stronger connection with the husband. However, it is always a tough call because it is like walking a tightrope, and making an informed decision about continuities can be difficult.

* * *

The decade of the 1990s became a time to think about, reflect on, and mourn the Holocaust. A similar time occurred in the 1960s that was triggered by, and resulted from, the capture and the trial of Adolf Eichmann. His very presence showed the world just what the Germans had done and how they went about carrying out the Final Solution.

In the 1990s there were several stimulants that came together: it was fifty years since the end of World War II, Holocaust survivors all over the world were rapidly aging, Holocaust deniers were emerging, and the brilliant Steven Spielberg's Holocaust film *Schindler's List* (1993) was released—all significant factors that came together to cause us to look at the Holocaust once again. A number of foundations all over the country banded together to expand The Shoah Visual History to make sure that the remaining fifty thousand Shoah survivors were never forgotten. To that end the Spielberg Foundation enlisted numerous volunteers all over the country to find survivors to be interviewed about their experiences and their survival of this horrible event.

In 1996 I was approached by Dr. Jack Graller, a psychiatrist and personal friend who was actively involved in this amazing project. There was something about his request that intrigued but also frightened me because I felt that I was expected to relive and reexperience my life during the Holocaust. When I mentioned this to family members, they were in favor of my participating, but I still hesitated even though I felt that I was moving closer to doing it.

In my dreams my anxieties were being replayed. Even though I agreed to do it, I did not feel relieved but instead became more anxious and difficult to live with. Even my young children noticed that I became moody and withdrawn.

My wife could not comprehend what my problem was; I was functioning well at my job and on the surface, I was doing what I was supposed to do on a daily basis. The week before the interview I had anxiety dreams every night—in those dreams I was being chased by German soldiers. I woke up at night with palpitations and drenched in sweat. Everyone was sleeping peacefully except me.

The night before the interview I stayed up most of the night trying to make an outline of what I would say. That morning Dr. Graller, a videographer with a huge camera, and an assistant appeared at my door.

My three children were also present, and my grandson was running around the house. I would not shake hands with anyone because my palms were so sweaty.

I was overly anxious and shaky during the beginning, talking too fast or being hesitant. However, after a while I got into a rhythm and felt somewhat relaxed and tense at the same time. Dr. Graller was excellent because as a psychiatrist he was experienced and professional in his manner. When he sensed an increase in my anxiety, he backed off. It was comforting being interviewed by a friend.

After my interview was over Dr. Graller asked the rest of the family to comment about what they heard about my experiences. They already knew a lot because, two years prior, we had a Seder during which I shared with them my experiences in detail.

So, I survived my second experience of the Holocaust and was able to sleep very soundly for the next few weeks. I did not appreciate just how tense I was, and subsequently experienced relief with a capital R!

* * *

Looking back on my life I cannot help but feel that I have been fortunate—perhaps lucky is a more accurate description. Luck is described as the chance happening of fortunate events. I was discussing my life with a friend some years ago and mentioned the fact that my wife is an excellent mother and a wonderful partner. He smiled and said that I must be lucky, and I responded that that was exactly how I felt. When I gave a talk once about how I survived the Holocaust a gentleman who listened intently to my story came up to me afterwards and said that the best way to describe my survival was as a miracle. The definition of a miracle is an event that seems impossible to explain by natural laws so it may be regarded as supernatural in origin. Each time I go back in my Holocaust history and rethink the chain of events that occurred those last few days before our liberation I am still unable to make sense of it, and perhaps never will. Being discovered by the Germans, their believing our story, not seeing the men hiding under the beds, accepting our explanation for choosing not to join them, not connecting the three men that ran out, and being bombarded by Russian artillery for several days without getting hurt or injured—all of these events are just unexplainable.

In my clinical work I have learned that many things happen in our lives that cannot be explained. One of our responsibilities as human beings is to try to explain the unexplainable. If we succeed in and are successful in that responsibility, it is very gratifying. If we fail it is frustrating and disappointing, yet we keep trying—that is what being human is all about. So, I plan to spend the rest of my life trying to figure out what happened to us, and why. It is a puzzle that demands a solution, even if a solution never comes.

INDEX

ABOUT THE AUTHOR

At the age of 84, Dr. Benjamin Garber continues to practice child and adult psychiatry and psychoanalysis full time. In addition to *A Child of the Ghetto*, he has written 30 clinical papers dealing with the impact of parent loss on children, as well as two books: *Follow-up Study of Hospitalized Adolescents* (1972) and *Psychoanalysis and Children* (Coeditor; 2009). He is a Training and Supervising analyst at the Chicago Psychoanalytic Institute, where he has worked with the Institute's Children's Grief Center (f/k/a Barr-Harris) since its inception, and served as its Director for 17 years. He currently serves as Director Emeritus. Dr. Garber and his wife, Wylie are parents to three accomplished children and have eight grandchildren.